May the Lord bless you with His presence and guide you with His grace.

J.D. M...

Permissions to use
previously published material
appear on page 174.

Published by

DeepRiver Books

a division of VMI Publishers
Sisters, Oregon
www.vmipublishers.com

ISBN: 1-933204-07-9
(ISBN-13: 9781933204079)
Library of Congress Control Number: 2005931341

Author Contact:
www.avoiceiscalling.com

COPYRIGHT © 2005 BY J.G. MARKING
(ALL RIGHTS RESERVED)

Dedication

For Christ,
Always.

Acknowledgements

Special thanks to my wonderful wife Jessica for all her love despite hours of forced readings over endless revisions • Thanks to my parents for always encouraging me to dream and for the knowledge that they will always be there • Thanks to my grandmother Donna for her support in so many ways too numerous and astounding to mention • Thanks to my brother Justin and best-friend Brent for their optimism and amity • Thanks to Nikki, Todd, Jackson, Jarrett and Fred for their warmth and endless smiles • Thanks to Jerry, Jessele, Jordan, Helen, Del, David and Jonathan for their familial kindness and thoughtfulness • Thanks to the Marking family for cherishing me and nurturing me no matter the distance • Thanks to the Gordon family for bestowing upon me the gift of their generosity and compassion • Thanks to all of my family especially for loving me so purely and affectionately • Thanks to all of my friends, you know who you are, for providing me with laughter and camaraderie when I've needed it the most • Thanks to my church for bearing my burdens, edifying me and inspiring me to more intimately seek God • Thanks to Bill, Lacey, Cathi and Marty for their inexhaustible understanding and stirring guidance • Thanks to the many authors who inspired me to pick up a pen • Thanks to my many teachers who taught me how to write • Thank you my reader, for the journey you're allowing me to share with you • Thank you Lord Jesus, for your unrelenting love, limitless grace and constant companionship.

Preface

There once was a man who lay in his bed and couldn't fall asleep at night.
No matter what he did, or thought in his head, nothing seemed quite right.
So as he thought and wondered what could possibly keep him awake,
His heart stilled and his mind silenced and he felt a gentle quake.
I want more.
And as his eyes opened wide his soul began to breathe,
A gentle whisper in his ear:
"I know what I heard with those simple three words,
But something's troubling me here.
However obvious those words may seem,
Their message isn't clearly defined.
Because I know, deep down in my soul…
The Voice that spoke wasn't mine."
"Who are You?" said the man whose heart had heard the breath divine.
"What is it that You want more of?" he asked with a tremor in his spine.
And as the moments passed and his pulse amplified,
He heard a word that would never leave his side.
Everything.
And as the man paused to contemplate,
This unwavering echo in his ear,
A subtle sense of bewilderment,
Crept in alongside fear.
"I know that the everything You want,
Includes all of my life that You see.
But what I have never realized 'til now,
Is that You offer Your everything—to me."

Contents

Introduction—Is This All There Is? 11
A Note from the Author 15

Part One: When Longing Meets the Living God

1. *Responding to the Calling Voice:*
   Abiding in the Light of God 19

Part Two: Actively Pursuing the Presence of God

2. *The Heart of Christianity—Prayer* 33
3. *"For My Eyes Have Seen the King": Worship* 45
4. *Man Can't Live on Bread Alone: The Word of God* 55
5. *Clinging to the Vine: Faith* 69

Part Three: Applying the Grace of God to Every Day Life

6. *Embracing Weakness for His Strength: Humility* 83
7. *To Each His Own: Forgiveness* 95
8. *Taking Up the Cross of Christ: Devotion* 105
9. *The Forgetting of Self: Service* 117

Part Four: Living a Life of Love—Becoming a Reflection of the Lord Jesus Christ

10. *The Family of God: Fellowship* 129
11. *And the Greatest of These Is: Love* 139
12. *Go: Evangelism* 149
13. *I AM With You Always: Discipleship* 159

Appendix: "Dearest Lord Jesus" 169
Index of Scriptures 170
Bibliography 172
Permissions 174

Introduction
Is This All There Is?

What do you really want from life? Is there something missing from your life that you can't quite put your finger on?

For some individuals this is a basic question and they don't give it much thought. They only cover the top layer of this issue and answer with the first thing that pops up into their mind like, "well, I'm still single…" or "I really want a new (fill in the blank with a possession)" or "I want to be successful."

Now these answers aren't necessarily bad ones, such as the desire for companionship or security and usually these answers are true but as you can see from a certain perspective, these answers are definitely not the remedy to an individual's yearning for something more from their life. These answers are the *indicator* of wanting something more, not the reasons for it. Or if we want to use medical terminology: these answers are only symptoms, not the ailment itself.

All of us yearn to be fulfilled, or better yet to acquire something that will eliminate our need for completion. Have you ever come across an individual who does not want something more out of their life? I haven't! We always seem to have a void inside us no matter how many ways we try to fill it. Something happens deep down in the core of our being at specific instances in our life that forces us to feel disturbingly empty no matter how much we achieve or acquire, no matter how much we have.

For example, immediately following my graduation from college I took a job that I thought would provide me with purpose (and income, to be quite honest) and yet I felt deeply hollow. Despite the salary, despite the benefits, and even despite the lucrative, enjoyable position, I wanted a "better" job.

So, I quit. And quickly began looking for my "better" job. Sure enough, a few weeks later I found a job I thought would finally fulfill my aching for a deeper, more profound existence and thus took it enthusiastically. But, as you probably can guess, within a few months my "better" job was quite obviously not the "best" job in my eyes and after the disappointment and disillusionment I experienced again I started looking elsewhere. And thus the cycle repeated.

As you can see, it really is a vicious cycle because the new job was not the source of my craving. If it were, my thirst for a fuller life would have ended when I found that "better" job. But it didn't. My yearning for the elusive, true and complete life grew exponentially. It was as if the job-switching quest highlighted the emptiness within me, instead of filling it. An example of this kind of misplaced quest for satisfaction is something we all suffer from: dry skin. No matter how much we scratch and scratch at itchy, dry skin, we will never be able to scrape away the irritation. The scratching only makes the cracked, flaky condition worse. So why do we continue scratching? Because we still itch! But ultimately we don't really want to scratch an itch. What we really desire is for *that itch to disappear*. This truth is lost to us as we scrape and writhe away.

It is only when we shift our perspective off of the ailment and onto the genuine remedy that we are able to apply lotion onto our broken skin and find relief. With this in mind, we must ask ourselves a new question: what is the genuine remedy for an unfulfilling and incomplete life?

What are you living for right now? What is your life about? If one thing defined your life, what would it be? You see, life, no matter the level of complexity or circumstance, can be summed into one defining statement- life is a pursuit. Our life truly is a pursuit of some ultimate "goal." Perhaps if we find out what we *have been* pursuing we may be able to find out why we're not experiencing fulfillment. What if the *thing* we have been pursuing with our life has contributed to our emptiness?

If we could only find what's actually *causing* our yearning for fulfillment instead, then maybe, just maybe, we might be able to solve all of the answers to the questions of, "What do I really want? What's missing from my life?"

Obviously what is missing from our lives can not be any possession because we keep on wanting things after we buy things (for instance, I've paid for my groceries, left the store and then returned to buy a chocolate bar ten seconds later because I saw someone else walking out with it).

And since most people feel that they can find security in an alarm system or bigger bank account, or find success in accomplishments, they are of course shocked to realize that after they acquire all of these things they still desire *bigger* and *better* things. We can be supremely confident, then, in the statement that the answer to our hunger is probably not something that we ourselves can ever obtain.

Upon hearing this a question immediately jolts into your head. "Well if I can't ever get what it is I'm missing or fix this problem, then how on earth will I ever find out what it is I really want? How will I ever find *my* remedy?" And that would be a good question. In fact it is the same question that every single human being has asked since the Garden of Eden, or better yet, since the loss of the Garden of Eden, of paradise. But ironically, it's not really paradise we're missing but rather what made paradise so heavenly.

If there is no possible way to fill that void and stop the longing, then why is it still there? Why did Alexander the Great desire to acquire more lands, wealth and power when he had already conquered more than any other man in history? Why did Rameses the II (for that matter why does anyone these days) desire the next best love and bride, after he already found a loving wife? Why did Icarus soar so close to the sun when he had already learned to fly?

Why can't that longing ever seem to be filled? Apparently the thing we really want is the thing we can't ever attain on our own. There is a longing in our heart, in our very soul, which we ourselves can't fill. So then maybe the reason that we want something more is not just our doing. If we can't obtain true fulfillment on our own, maybe something else is taking place deep down in our very being that makes us always want something more. Something, or someone, is missing from our lives and cries out to us, beckons us, calls us to keep searching. And the Answer to all of this can only be: God.

Since we can't find fulfillment by obtaining anything ourselves that is of *this* world, then the only rational, logical answer is that we long for something *not* of this world. God alone is what can possibly fill us, complete us. God alone is the one thing we can't obtain from *this* world.

God *is* calling us, but for what?

A Note from the Author

No matter where you are in your walk or relationship with the Lord, or even if you don't believe in Him, He is beckoning you to come closer and take His hand at this very instant. He is inviting you to come and experience completeness because only through Him will your life be made whole. All have felt the nudge of God, all have heard the call of Christ. So, how will you respond?

I encourage you to take the first step of filling the God-shaped hole in your life right now and ask Jesus to come into your life, forgive your sins and save you. If the answer to our longing is getting closer to God during our daily lives and since there can be no getting close to God because of our sin, except through Jesus Christ and His sacrifice, love and grace, we must receive the gift of redemption. (In Appendix A there is a prayer I prayed that helped me find salvation through Christ if you are serious about living the fulfilling life in Christ). A Voice is calling you to actively and authentically pursue the presence of Almighty God.

My hope is to provide you with a fresh, new perspective on why you feel incomplete in life sometimes, what your relationship with God truly is, what the Christian life truly means and what your life in Christ and on this earth is meant to be. This book is designed to provide you with the way to become whole- the transforming touch of the Living Christ. My aim is to present you with Bible-tested and Spirit-driven ways to live in the presence of God, and by doing so, become more like Christ—which makes you truly come alive!

I hope this time we share together will not only heal your heart and continually inspire you along the journey, but I hope that it draws your life into the very presence of Almighty God. And through His transforming hands you can grab hold of the life He gave for you.

But let me ask you a question first:

What are *you* going to do? What are *you actually going to do* about your desire for the New Life found in Christ?

As we all know, deep down, the only thing that can change and better our life is our own response to the call of God. You are the one living your life, therefore only you can solve or change anything. Only you make the decisions and choices in your life that will edify you or cripple you, enlighten you or lead you astray, damn you or save you. A piece of paper, no matter how pretty or poignant, is not going to provide you with peace, comfort, purpose or salvation. It can't. Only you can go about actually doing the things that lead to a new life, the New Life.

Now the breath of life and life itself comes from God, and the New Life does as well but only you can accept or reject that Life; no one else can do it for you no matter what anyone else may tell you. Ultimately, when the gift of life is graciously laid before you, you are the only one who can accept it or refuse it. And you accept or deny this gift by the life you live and the choices you make or don't make, the things you believe or don't believe.

So, when it comes to this book providing you with an exciting and exhilarating new life filled with wonder, splendor and a peace that surpasses all understanding, I can safely promise you that this book will do absolutely none of that! But you can. With the help and intercession of the Holy Spirit of God, you can embrace all the things that you have been promised. And this book can help *equip* you to do so.

It will provide you with the encouragement that you really can experience an authentic and God-overflowing life, equip you with the perspectives, tools and knowledge of how to go about living your life in a way that leads to an authentic experience with God. This book will daily inspire you to seek the Source of a passionate, comforting and exhilarating life- the very presence of Jesus Christ.

A Voice is calling each of us to come and experience daily — the touch of the Living God. Are you ready to go on this expedition together? (Go ahead, I'll give you some time to think it over)…

Fantastic!

Let's go!

PART ONE

When Longing Meets the Living God

Chapter One

Responding to the Calling Voice: Abiding in the Light of God

> *"A voice is calling, clear the way for the Lord in the wilderness; make smooth in the desert a highway for our God. Let every valley be lifted up, and every mountain and hill be made low; and let the rough ground become a plain, and the glory of the Lord will be revealed, and all flesh will see it together; for the mouth of the Lord has spoken."*
> —Isaiah the Prophet

> *"Everyone who is of the truth hears My voice…
> I have come as Light into the world, so that everyone who believes in me will not remain in darkness…I AM the Light of the world; he who follows me will not walk in darkness, but will have the Light of life."*
> –Jesus of Nazareth

Have you ever had to walk great distances outside in the winter? During my university days I vividly remember that I had to park far away from campus and trek to my classes because all the close spots were always taken. The sheer distance I had to walk was, no lie, two miles…in the snow, uphill both ways… okay just two miles. In north central Oklahoma during the winter months when the temperature drops to the teens there's not a whole lot to help you escape a thirty mile per hour wind that feels like tiny ice needles on every area of exposed skin.

So during my trek to class I would desperately avoid any and all buildings, trees or even light posts. Seriously, I would keep at least a twenty to thirty foot distance from them. Why? Simple: their shadows blocked the sun. The cold, long walk was bearable when I was bathed in the light and warmth of the sun. In fact sometimes, despite the unpleasant nature of my circumstance and the hostile temperatures of the season, the journey was quite lovely.

Such is the Christian life. How many of us feel like we are under the overcast skies of a brutal winter and can't seem to find our place in the sun? In my experiences as a minister and friend I have come to find that most followers of Christ feel, at one time or another, that their Christian walk is inadequate or lacking; even worse they don't know what to do or how to fix it. So they are left feeling empty, as though they are living only a shell of the real Christian life they have been called by God to live, the life they are meant to live.

This is a serious problem that has the potential to affect many, if not all, disciples of Christ. You see, once our soul has felt the touch of the Living God we will always want more. Once we come to know God we want to know more of God. That is why we feel comfort and assurance of salvation, yet desire more. We, as Christ's disciples, genuinely desire to grow and experience an abundant life in Christ but always seem to fall short. Many of us who follow Christ feel trapped in the inescapable quicksand of a mediocre life that is rapidly dragging us down into the depths of dissatisfaction, the abyss of apathy.

"What can I do to live an abundant life in Christ?"

The only way to stay on the journey, the only way to ever enjoy this journey of life we have to venture on in this often icy, dreary world is the Light of God. The secret to a life of following Christ, abiding in the Light of God, embodies a relationship, a continuous closeness, a daily dependence upon and devotion to Jesus, not a one-time designation. And right here is where the true life of following Christ begins or ends. Do we choose to foster a real relationship with Christ and make Him the spark of all our dreams and doings? Do we choose to put abiding in His presence as our utmost priority and aim *or* do we focus more on performing religious rituals than becoming His disciple?

And that choice is ultimately yours. If you focus on a relationship with God, you can grow. The possibilities of loving God with everything you are and loving your neighbors as yourself are endless because you choose to become as He is, life itself. But, if you choose religious rituals you choose numbness and a limited growth in your walk with Christ. You will only be performing empty services which in and of themselves can't mold you into the likeness of Christ; only the Hands of God can. If you don't have a relationship with Him and only have your rituals, like "church" or good deeds, then you simply don't have God. You just have you and your "hollow" actions.

When you become a child of God it's not like you just put your life on autopilot and coast through existence. That's not a life God wants for you! I'm not even sure that can be classified as living. The event of giving Christ your life must happen every single time you step out on that road called life.

This is why we must *tirelessly* and with *relentless concentration* keep ourselves turning to Christ for navigational guidance. If we don't then can we really ever expect to reach the destination He desires for us? But how can we authentically and passionately pursue the presence of God in a way that will empower and invigorate us to live the life He desires us to live? Or in other words, "in what ways can I pursue His presence throughout my daily life?"

The key to pursuing God's presence every day is to invite God into your presence every day. That sounds too simple and too easy. Well it is quite simple and yet, not at all easy. But let me emphasize that this Biblical truth is not *too* simple. There is no weird and intricate process we must perform to seek the Lord's presence. As James 4:8 beautifully states:

"Draw near to God; and He will draw near to you."

Herein lays the simplicity and the difficulty. The simplicity is that our relationship with God, like our relationship with anyone else, will only be as close or distant as we make it. And it is in this that we find the difficulty. Our relationship with God grows or diminishes based entirely on our effort to make our relationship with God an intimate and vibrant one.

Many disciples become stagnant and disappointed in their walk with God because they fail to include the grace and Spirit of Christ into their everyday life. They focus solely on godlier living and forget the Living God. We sometimes expect God to do all the pursuing and forget what He tells us in Proverbs 8:17:

"Those who *diligently* seek me—will find me" (emphasis added).

Not seeing our relationship with God as an actual living, breathing relationship results in a cold, calculated Christianity where only actions are performed instead of cultivating intimacy. We are prone to view Christianity in a merit-based way because of our competitive and performance driven temperament. We naturally tend to focus upon accomplishments and attaining some ultimate goal when it comes to getting "close" to God instead of fostering a personal relationship with Jesus. In reality we're not focusing on getting close to God when we associate Christianity with performance, but rather on our own "godliness"; we have lost touch with the true reason for our existence, knowing Christ.

We really have a tendency to turn this whole "Be holy, for I AM holy" thing into an exercise plan of "achieving" salvation instead of embarking on a never-ending conversation and commitment to Christ. It's almost silly, but we really are competitive creatures out to not only achieve, but outshine and surpass everyone around us, which unfortunately often includes the Lord! Many individuals attribute this to the age old sin of pride, of which I will agree usually but, I also think that in this modern age we are more oriented to believe that growth can only be documented through outward calculations than in any other moment in history.

One of the things that this cold and calculating method of thought has crippled is one of the most vital aspects of Christianity: The importance of the unseen, unheard and incalculable transformation of the human heart when coming face to face with God.

Art, poetry, epic stories, music and the kiss of a loved one have no scientific measurement or calculable worth. But all of us who have been moved by a painting, touched by a poem, caught up in a grand adventure, brought to tears by a song and forever changed by the kiss of one we love, know that some things can't be measured, only treasured.

The Key to Abiding in the Light of God

As we've discussed, emotional and spiritual growth can not always be measured outwardly. How you treat others and your devotion to the spiritual disciplines (time spent in prayer, reading Scripture, etc.) can sometimes show others and yourself how committed you are to fostering and sustaining a relationship with God. However, in other situations, only the inward movement of the Holy Spirit can lead you out of the shadows and into the warm rays of a closer walk with Him.

Sometimes to grow in a relationship with God we have to throw away the outward actions and activities that we all use to gauge how "spiritual" we are and return to the purpose of these activities- getting closer to the side of Jesus Christ. But actions are all we know, all we've been taught.

So instead of concerning ourselves with the intangible and incalculable thing called a relationship with God, we instinctively begin to center our walk with Christ on the things that we can count and tally, such as how much of the Bible we read or how often we attend church. Or like true competitors, we may compare our walk with God on how much better or worse we are than Sally, or John or Paul.

Our entire relationship with God can quickly become dependent upon and even based on comparisons to someone else's visible "pursuit" of God. And any time you're comparing yourself, holiness or spirituality wise, with someone else to determine how strong your walk with God is, you're missing the picture of what a relationship really is- uniquely divine.

My walk with the Lord Jesus will not be exactly like anyone else's on this earth so how then can I compare or judge my "holiness" to another's? I can't. Which is one of the reasons I believe Christ urged us to "not judge so that you will not be judged" –Matthew 7:1. Ultimately, the only individual you will be compared to in your lifetime is one person: Jesus Christ. And to judge another is to give him free reign to compare our lives to Christ's.

Also, anytime you place visible aspects of holiness above the invisible moving of the Holy Spirit within you, you lose touch with the very Spirit of God you hope to experience. Any action not saturated with God's very hand, no matter how visibly good it may be, is worthless because God is not in it and throughout it. Do we like this truth? No, of course not. We want to be able to produce good and noble things all on our own. We don't like the idea that we can do nothing of merit or worth without God. And it's true. We can't because of our fallen and selfish nature.

But as Philippians 4:13 so beautifully tells us, despite the fact that we can do nothing without God:

"I can do all things through Christ who strengthens me."

Now I'm all for diving wholeheartedly into the Word of God (which you will definitely see in later chapters or already see through the bounty of Scriptures already quoted) and attending church, but unfortunately these are not always true pictures of how someone's relationship with God is going. So we've really got to get this out of our heads that Christianity is about how often we attend church or how much of the Bible we know. God is much more concerned with how much of the Bible is in your heart and present in your life than how much of it is just in your head.

And since Christianity is not just about actions, but about Christ and a relationship with Him, many individuals miss out on the Christ of Christianity (the person) and focus only on the human effort aspect of it (the deeds). We almost make ourselves out to be the center of Christianity through the "importance and grandeur" of our endeavors or our track record. It's almost as if we are not really seeking Christ, but seeking emotion-manufacturing activities. We don't seek Christ in worship; we seek worship so that it will manifest Christ to us. In other words, we seek worship so that we can experience the feeling of Christ's presence, instead of seeking His presence despite feeling anything at all.

Do you see how this is completely backwards?

Seek Him, and only Him. Religion can not bring us the relationship with God that we pine after, only Jesus can. Attending church *can be* an outward representation of our inward commitment to seeking God. But unfortunately for many people attending church is more habit than hunger for God. Likewise with reading the Bible. In fact, reading the Word of God does not always indicate a passionate pursuit of God because reading itself doesn't transform you, Christ does. So if all you're doing is reading and not seeking the very face and heart of Christ in your reading then you can't expect transformation or growth in your relationship with the Lord. (This will be discussed further in a later chapter.)

Instead of focusing on abiding in the Light of God we try to manufacture our own twisted form of "light" onto our lives. We wield our tiny flashlight and unintentionally believe we have or even *are* the light now. But any light we might think we have possesses neither warmth nor illumination. In essence, we just don't see what we're doing. And there is where we discover our mistake, the age-old mistake of trying to control the uncontrollable: God.

If we don't have an authentic view of what following Christ looks like and don't realize what a relationship with God must be, our passion and devotion for Jesus will diminish in the shadows of discouragement because we will fail to enter into the presence of Christ.

The key to conquering this is to grasp the reality that Christ and Christianity are not about what you do, but who He is and how you can seek Him. Living for Christ means inviting Christ to be not only your Savior, which is usually not the difficult part, but to be your Lord. Lords ruled, and yes, even commanded their subjects in the ways to live and what to do—every day. And to truly be Christ (Healer and Redeemer) He must be both. You can't have Jesus Christ as your Savior if He is not Jesus Christ your Lord. You can't have one without the other.

The Three Truths We Must Understand About Living the Christian Life

But before we learn about the ways in which we can pursue the presence of God in our daily lives, there are three truths we must understand about the daily Christian life first. The three truths are: we must correct our unrealistic and incorrect expectations about the Christian life; we must realize the combination that desire and discipline produces (discipleship); and we must truly become a new creation with a new (second) nature.

THE FIRST TRUTH: WE HAVE UNREALISTIC AND INCORRECT EXPECTATIONS OF WHAT THE CHRISTIAN LIFE IS SUPPOSED TO BE AND WHY GOD MADE US, THAT NEED TO BE CORRECTED.

Unrealistic and incorrect expectations about the Christian life as a source of problems in our spiritual growth should not really surprise any of us since we commonly set up unrealistic expectations for ourselves and then become discouraged and almost angry at the fact that *our* expectations have not been met in the exact way in which we wanted them to be. The most devastating of these false expectations and ideas we have about the Christian life centers around how we go about pursuing the presence of God.

Too many times we get so wrapped up in the routine motions of the daily grind that we can't seem to find time for God or are unwilling to *give up* "our time" to insert Christ into our busy schedule. We lose touch with God because we have not put Him first in our lives. In all truth, many of us do not have God as our god. We place work in the position of god, or we place family there, or money there or some other "thing" as our god instead of the true and living Lord! And then we don't understand why we feel so distant from Christ!

Many of us must realize sooner or later that when we give our lives to Christ and make Him Lord, we are the ones who must keep Him there. Christ will only be Lord of your life when you *make* Him God of your life. We all too often try to slip some time with the Lord in between dinner and bedtime or before our day really begins and lose sight of the fact that the entire day is God's!

Instead of making time for God throughout our day we really ought to make our *entire day* for God since *time* is His, our very *life* is His. This means keeping our thoughts fixed upon serving and seeking the Lord no matter the situation. Whether at home, at work or in line at a department store, we must keep our focus upon Jesus Christ or else everything will suddenly become unclear. The key is not to fit Christ into your busy life; it's to place your entire life, no matter how busy, into Christ.

And yet this will not and does not come easy to any of us.

The Second Truth: Only when desire meets discipline, can discipleship transform us.

If we are to ever have a vibrant relationship with our Lord and live the life of hope and purpose He has for us, then we must know and pursue the ways in which we can live in the presence of God. And since many followers of Christ yearn for an exhilarating and intimate walk with God, but just don't know how to turn that desire into daily discipleship, there's no wonder that so many of us grow frustrated and disenchanted. So because of our stagnant disappointment, many believers feel that the abundant and fruitful life of following Christ is an unattainable illusion and end up settling for lukewarm living. We handcuff ourselves to a mediocre spirituality that we desperately want to escape.

The stark reality that this very thing is happening to believers and children of God at this moment throughout the world is more than sad; it's sinister. Followers of Christ become so disappointed because of the daunting promise that they can become like Christ that when they mess up they deem the life of a believer as impossible and give up. The voice of Christ that summons each of us is not only an invitation to a New Life but a request to come and share a life of intimacy and deep friendship with God. Christ doesn't just demand a relationship with you, He eagerly awaits your company so His strength can lift you up to become like Him despite all your setbacks and failures.

And in doing so, whenever you seek the face of God with all your heart (*desire*) in whatever you do, no matter what your circumstances or situation (*discipline*), you allow yourself to become one step closer to daily *discipleship*, one step closer to Christ. If we follow Christ passionately while on earth,

He will mold us into His image of perfection throughout all of eternity. But what we forget is that eternity does not just include then and there, but here and now. We will never achieve perfection this side of heaven, but we can become more like Christ through His divine grace and guidance every day we live!

We all must constantly remember that the Holy Spirit of God is not only alive in our heart, but at work in our lives. In Jesus Christ the Holy Spirit of God becomes a real-life, actual Guide and Companion, as Brennan Manning proclaims:

John declares, 'Eternal life is this: to know you, the only true God, and Jesus Christ whom you have sent' (John 17:3). God's love becomes flesh and blood in the person of Jesus. In Him it receives hands and feet, a face, and a voice [...] The power of His Spirit passes into my Spirit and the purpose of Pentecost is fulfilled—Christ is formed within me not just in peak moments of transcendental experience but in the nitty gritty of daily life.[1]

Since this is true, why do so many of us abandon the very spiritual disciplines that can help foster the vibrant relationship with God we so deeply crave? Well one answer is that we fail at doing them. We fail at not only utilizing the spiritual disciplines at our disposal, but we even fail in wanting to use them. I know I do! But the ironic thing is that we desire to *want* to do them. We *want* to have the desire in us to always pursue the Lord in any way we can.

We wish that we did want to always seek His face in prayer without ceasing and be patient and worship Him in all we do, in spirit and truth. But for some reason we don't. We don't always want to give up that television show or sporting event or trip to the mall for some quiet time with the Lord. I mean, we want—to want—to pursue the presence of God in our daily lives, but we can't seem to turn that desire into fruitful action.

So why are all of these things so hard? Why can't we just naturally feel motivated and inspired to always seek His face? Why don't all of our bad habits and temptations to sin just vanish once we start following Christ? Why doesn't holiness just ooze out of every pore of our body the moment Christ is made Lord of our life?

Well, because you're human. You're a *fleshly* creature shooting for a *spiritual* righteousness in Christ. Change is a difficult process that is never easy, especially when your aim is perfection, which is precisely what Christ has called us to be.

THE THIRD TRUTH: IT'S NEVER EASY TO BECOME WHAT YOU'VE NEVER BEEN: TRULY BECOMING A NEW CREATION WITH A NEW (SECOND) NATURE.

"Though youths grow weary and tired, and vigorous young men stumble badly, yet those who wait for the Lord will gain new strength; they will mount up with wings like eagles, they will run and not get tired, they will walk and not become weary." –Isaiah 40:30-31.

This life of following God has been and always will be difficult because it's completely foreign to us. The path of holiness and life in the Spirit is completely foreign to us because we are not holy or spirit; we are fallen and flesh. Now when we give our lives to Christ, the Holy Sprit of God does come to dwell in our hearts and hallelujah for that wonderful gift! But that does not mean that our flesh disappears or that our responsiveness to the desires of the flesh vanish (which, to be honest, would be extremely beneficial but is obviously not a reality while we still live on earth).

We are sensual beings—as in we relate to our environment and world through touch, sight, sound, taste and smell. Therefore one of the reasons that the Christian life is so hard for us is because we are called to live a life in the Spirit and not in the flesh. But unfortunately we are still encased in flesh! We have the Lord's Spirit alive and empowering us but we still have a tendency to revert back to our five-sense way of living. We want to live in the flesh and respond only to the tangible world because that is all we have known; that's where we feel *comfortable*.

In addition, any act of righteousness or divine breathings will always be contrary to our nature because we are not righteous or divine by our very nature at all; we are fallen sinners. Does this take away from the saving grace of God and the glory and wonder of salvation in Christ? No! Never in a million years! But what it *does* do is eliminate the misconception that the Christian road to holiness and a closer walk with Christ is an easy, natural process. It's not! As the Word of God clearly tells us the straight and narrow path has been and always will be the most difficult life you can ever lead because it involves you going against every single one of your natural, instinctive tendencies.

This is exactly like trying to break a life-long habit that you know is detrimental to your well being. No matter how much you know you shouldn't be doing it, you just can't seem to stop engaging in that habit because, by golly, you've always been doing it. It's what you know. And in the case of habitual sin, it's not only hauntingly familiar to you and easy to fall back into, it's treacherously tempting.

In fact, sometimes you can be so used to a habit that you can't even really wrap your mind around what a life without that habit could be or would even look like. You can't see a life without the habit because you can't remember the moments in your life when you existed and survived while not doing your habit. (Cracking my knuckles, back, neck, well let's face it anything I can get to pop, has been an annoying and troublesome habit that I never can quite seem to break fully, yet).

But here is where you must see that the life of Christ will never be natural to your habitual way of fleshly living. To live your life in the Spirit you must constantly be at war with the fallen, fleshly part of you that consistently rebels against the Jesus within your heart. Holiness and a life in the Spirit will never come naturally to you, which is why, with the help of Almighty God, you must *make it second nature*.

The Three Things You Can Do to Break an Unwanted Habit

In my ministerial experiences I have found that there are three things you can do, in fact must do, to successfully break an unwanted habit and help yourself live a life of second nature. And an unwanted habit is precisely what living in the flesh is. That's all that it is! A sinful and tempting habit that we must break with the aid of His Spirit to live for the glory of Christ!

>1. STOP THINKING ABOUT THE IMPOSSIBILITY OF ENDING THE HABIT.
>YOU MUST HAVE HOPE AND CONFIDENCE THAT YOU CAN DEFEAT IT.

Luckily, "With God, all things are possible." Matthew 19:26. This is one of the foundations of any faith we have in the Christian life, to become in Christ what we can not become on our own: Holy. Christ made you a promise that if you gave Him everything and followed Him, He would make you like Himself and bring you to eternal life with the Father.

Believe it. And take hold of His promise. As discussed earlier, if you base your walk with God around anything other than Him the hope of becoming more like Christ seems to grow increasingly impossible because you just can't stop messing up. Since the New Life seems impossible, you stop pursuing the very tools (spiritual disciplines) that the Father has given you to use; under the right motives and through daily devotion these tools can actually help you live the abundant life of Christ.

This leads us into our next aid.

>2. SURROUND YOURSELF WITH THINGS THAT CAN
>MAKE IT EASIER ON YOU TO FIGHT THE UNWANTED HABIT
>AND PURSUE YOUR NEW, DESIRED WAY OF LIVING.

It's excruciatingly easy to allow the negative events of life to cloud and distort the truth of how important it is to pursue the spiritual disciplines that help us become more like Christ and live a life in the Spirit (like prayer, worship, reading Scripture, etc.). One of the truly decimating things to a believer is the incorrect idea that the spiritual disciplines are not lifelines to Him at all, but rather are tedious chores or unessential to connecting with God.

When you surround yourself with the gifts that He has given us so that we may draw close to Him, the life of the Spirit doesn't seem too far off because the very Spirit of God is not far off; He overflows out of your heart. The spiritual disciplines are as essential to a relationship with God as food is to the body or gasoline is to your car.

Do any of us really think that way anymore? Well if we don't, we had better start. Because if we don't see prayer and faith and humility and Scripture as the food of God and fruits of the Vine then can we really ask ourselves why it seems so hard to become like Him? If we don't use what He has given us to do so, what do we expect?

Can we really ask ourselves, or God, why we're hungry for more? This leads us, very simply, into the last aid for breaking the chains of our fallen life and abiding in the Light of God.

3. ONCE YOU HAVE SURROUNDED YOURSELF WITH THE THINGS AND TOOLS THAT CAN AID YOU IN YOUR BATTLE TO OVERCOME YOUR DETRIMENTAL BEHAVIOR...

USE THEM!

Using a flat-head screwdriver to fix a sink with a loose flat-head screw is not a very difficult decision, right? Yet, it's funny how easily we overlook the simplest of truths like using the right tool for the job. You can't grow up to be big and strong if you don't eat your vegetables. And you can't grow closer to Christ if you don't nourish yourself with the food of the Spirit: entering into the presence of God.

In the chapters to come, you will be given applicable tools and insight into the twelve ways that you can genuinely pursue the presence of God in your daily life through the spiritual disciplines. And through each of these spiritual disciplines described in Scripture you can begin to live your life in the Spirit and come alive in Christ. Your Heavenly Father waits to bless you with the power and glory of His companionship today and every day of your life!

So let's go!

Application:

Immediately following each chapter in this book, like the one you just read, there will be an application for real life relevance and everyday integration.

There is space below this application section for you to write out and reassess your relationship, or for some of you to initiate a genuine relationship, with the Lord. You may start with "I would like my relationship with the Lord to be..." or even "Lord, I want to..." The honest-to-goodness consideration about your relationship with Christ is what is important here, not scribbling the "right" words. What do you desire from God?

What thoughts moved you in this chapter? After reading this chapter, do you think that you have had unrealistic thoughts or expectations about the Christian life?

Are you excited? (No writing necessary.)
I am! I can't wait for you to turn the next page!

Prayer:

Most gracious and loving Heavenly Father, thank You for loving us and relentlessly pursuing us with the life You have for us and desire us to live: a life of joy in You. We thank You for always granting us the opportunity to seek Your face and presence and promising us that You will draw near to us as we draw near to You. Thank You for Your Son, Jesus Christ, who is our guide and companion in this life so that we might better know You, serve You and love You Father, which will enable us to better know, serve and love each other as well. Give us, Lord, the clarity and strength to no longer cling to our unrealistic expectations and thus distance ourselves from Your side. Lord, grant us the strength to conquer our temptations and susceptibilities to the flesh and cling to the life in the Spirit, the true life of fulfillment found in Jesus. Father God, enable us to use the tools You have given us to help us experience Your Spirit daily. Guide us in all truth, Father God, and bless us with Your Holy Spirit so that we will not only read about how we can seek Your presence in the next twelve chapters, but passionately pursue You through them. We love You, Lord, and hunger only to know You better and to experience more of Your presence in our daily lives. We ask all of these things in the precious and powerful name of Jesus and for His sake always. Amen!

PART TWO

Actively Pursuing the Presence of God

Chapter Two

The Heart of Christianity: Prayer

"The Lord has heard my supplication, the Lord receives my prayer."
—Psalm 6:9

"In addition to all the other work that gets done through prayer, perhaps the greatest work of all is the knitting of the human heart together with the heart of God." [2]
—John Ortberg

I was dominating the basketball court. It was one of those few, monumental moments in a man's life when he can stop and say, "I'm actually not embarrassing myself right now in this athletic endeavor." I was a madman, a man possessed with the essence of Michael Jordan and Kareem all wrapped up into my five foot, nine inch frame. I couldn't miss a shot. I stole the ball nearly every time my man dribbled and I didn't taunt or revel in my obvious domination (a fact I was quite *proud* of at that moment—which now makes me question which is worse).

So as the opposing players around me were asking each other to switch and guard me, ("I can't stop this guy," one of them said as he gasped for air), a Cheshire smirk crept across my face and I flew towards the basket. As I soared through the air I let the ball go at the perfect height with a flawless arc and floated gracefully back to earth.

Or so I thought.

Loud pop.

Quickly followed by pain.

Unbelievable pain!!!

I had landed on an opposing player's foot and completely rolled my left ankle once over.

"Dude," the opposing player asked, "was that loud pop—your ankle?"

Great. He heard the pop...probably not a good sign there, Bud, I thought. (I've noticed that people talk to themselves upon injury, like when you stub your toe and then say out loud to yourself, "That really hurt." Obviously you already know it hurt...so who are you really talking to then?).

I lay there writhing in pain, rolling to and fro in obvious agony, and people just watched me like I was the wounded wildebeest on a hunting trip documentary. Luckily a trainer who was in the gym broke the safari-viewing and helped me get to the hospital where after an hour I was released to go home and my roommates carted me away from the Emergency Room.

So as I hobbled on my crutches looking like a new-born deer into my room I could feel the pain medication they had given me begin to fade away. I couldn't take anymore because I had already taken my full prescription, but it wasn't working. That night, as I lay uncomfortably in bed, desperately urging sleep to overtake me, I thought, "Okay, so what are you going to do about this God?"

All I could feel was the throbbing sting of my softball-sized ankle. Yet, all I could think about was *why aren't you helping me Jesus?* I passionately appealed God to remove or at least dull the pain so I could get a little sleep. Nothing. I began to grow weary, desperate and extremely agitated. Why is it that all illnesses and pains are worse at night? I began to grit my teeth and whimper as I said, "Please Jesus, take this pain from me. I need you to do this for me!" Nothing.

"I need you to show me that you love me. I need an answer!"

Nothing.

"Where are you? Why won't you do this for me? Why won't you reveal yourself and give me what I want, what I need?"

Silence.

As tears of frustration burned my cheeks, I began to slowly calm down and rest in the arms of my Father. It was only in this moment, my moment of complete surrender, that I felt a moving in my heart, a gentle whisper, an overwhelming comfort. And I knew it was God.

"Do not seek answers my child, seek Me."

"I *am* your Answer."

"I *am* the Answer."

My breathing slowed and the pain lifted ever so slightly. The crying had only begun.

C.S. Lewis once said, and I paraphrase, "pain is God's megaphone." [3] In that case, I am extremely hard of hearing.

Have *you* ever been in so much physical pain, like my ankle sprain incident, that you could barely think straight or that you began to wonder, *why did this really, really have to happen? How does this help me with my walk with you Lord? What are You going to do now to remove me from this pain?*

In retrospect, I find the events of that night especially indicative of human nature. I prayed only when I had used up all of my own limited abilities. I turned to Christ as a last resort instead of keeping in constant communion with my friend and Lord. What a sad commentary on how prayer is sometimes viewed. Isn't it heartbreaking that the majority of our prayers are usually reactive instead of proactive? We usually only turn to God after something happens, instead of putting Him first, which is where His Word tells us He belongs.

It, of course, was not the injury itself that brought about the shift in my heart and the gradual epiphany that always follows an encounter with the presence of God. It was the moment that God made Himself known to me that my entire viewpoint changed. As with most things that draw you closer to the Father, that injury was simply the opportunity that the Holy Spirit had to lower my defenses and remove the concerns that distracted me from Him. That injury shifted my focus off of my desires and selfishness and left me longing for the touch of the Father.

The Spirit left me quiet, suffering and defenseless before my God.

The essence of prayer, the very spirit of prayer, is to seek the Lord not for a transformation of our circumstances, but a transformation of ourselves through His presence. It's the greatest blessing that a Holy God can bestow upon His children. The more time I spend with the Lord in prayer the more I realize I'm not focusing on my wants at all. In fact, I'm not even focusing on myself, but on pursuing His righteousness.

All I could focus on was Christ the rest of that evening. Whether softly singing songs of praise or just talking to Jesus as if He was right next to me, (which He is, He is with us always), I didn't realize that I was, through prayer, being transformed into His likeness. Through prayer my heart began to mesh with the heart of Christ.

I began to see that prayer intrinsically forces you to submit your life and offer yourself to God (bowing your knee is symbolic of this) and focus solely upon the grace of Christ. When you pray you completely rely upon that which you do not see and that which you have no authority over: *God*. Prayer transforms us—not situations. Prayer does change our lives, but not by changing our circumstances. Prayer transforms our lives—by changing us.

Prayer is faith in action.

The Threefold Promise of Pro-active Prayer.

How do you approach prayer in your daily life? Is it out of an unquenchable desire to be one with the Father, the Son and the Holy Spirit? Or, like my ankle injury, is it a petition to a distant and all-powerful benefactor?

A follower of Christ must remember that asking from the Lord is not the sole or central purpose and power behind prayer. Receiving His blessings is a great and wonderful result of prayer, but obtaining gifts from God is not the reason we pray. Prayer is an active pursuit of God's presence and *transforming* touch. Speaking to Almighty God is not like distantly requesting a loan that may or may not happen. Prayer is meant to be a pro-active engagement with Jesus, not always a reactive and desperate "last resort."

"Rejoice always; pray without ceasing; in everything give thanks; for this is God's will for you in Christ Jesus," says 1 Thessalonians 5:16-18. Unfortunately though, the majority of prayer that I have lifted up to the Lord in my life is in response to some event or circumstance that I did not appreciate and wanted God to "correct", instead of a continual and endless communion with God.

I know many Christians who suffer the same disconnection from the Lord in their daily walk. The saddest part is that we do it to ourselves. God doesn't leave us; we just ignore Him usually until we're in a bind. We desire a change in our *circumstances*, not in ourselves.

But that misunderstanding about prayer is not the most devastating thing to our walk with God, not even close. The most destructive thought about prayer in the minds of many believers these days is the fact that at times, or every day, we wonder deep down, *does prayer really make a difference?*

When did prayer stop being the very power of God in our world? I know why most people only pray when they are in dire straits. It's simple: they don't really believe prayer changes things but when they've tried everything else, why not try prayer? If you don't really, deep down, have faith that prayer is the vehicle through which you change lives, then why do it unless everything else has failed?

You never know, I guess it could work.

No, prayer does not work that way. The life of Christ can not work that way. Not believing that the Lord Jesus actually meets us where we are when we pray results in the severing of our lives from the Vine.

"The idea that everything would happen exactly as it does regardless of whether we pray or not is a specter that haunts the minds of many who sincerely profess belief in God. It makes prayer psychologically impossible, replacing it with dead ritual at best." –Dallas Willard [4]

Prayer is not and must not be a "dead formality," as Dallas Willard warned us. Prayer is the heartbeat of Christianity. We all must look with new, revitalized eyes at the meaning and necessity of prayer. Every child of God can experience the transforming touch of God by understanding and applying the three truths of prayer, communion with God, to their daily lives.

Thanks to an ankle injury and the Holy Spirit's unrelenting love, *the purpose of prayer, the influence of prayer* and *the reality of prayer* helped transform my walk with Christ.

The Purpose of Prayer

"Prayer is the central avenue God uses to transform us...The closer we come to the heartbeat of God, the more we desire to be conformed to Christ."
—Richard Foster, Celebration of Discipline [5]

I have always adored the analogy of "I am the potter, you are the clay." If you've never had the opportunity to witness a sculptor turn a lump of clay into an immaculate lifelike sculpture, it's really quite breathtaking. The Father does the same with us. When we come to Him in the beginning of our walk, we are truly a lump of clay. We are unformed, fresh and our lives do not resemble anything close to the likeness of God's image because we have not yet intimately known Him.

But each time we go to the Lord in prayer and supplication, the healing and transforming touch of His hands presses on us, molding us, forming His own face into our human clay. The more we pursue His presence the more we begin to resemble the Lord Jesus and more incredibly, the more others can recognize Christ within us.

But if we try to mold ourselves into the likeness of Christ through godly actions, without seeking God, we end up just twisting ourselves around with no purpose or vision to follow. Including God in your every movement is the only way to *ever* become godly because only God can make us godly through His righteousness. If God is not included, everything we do is ultimately just actions "striving after the wind" as Ecclesiastes tells us.

"Thus I considered all my activities which my hands had done and the labor which I had exerted, and behold all was vanity and striving after wind and there was no profit under the sun" –Ecclesiastes 2:11.

One of the best examples of how prayer affects a child of God is the story of Moses in Exodus 34:29-35. Moses did not just resemble the inward likeness of God after communion with the Almighty, he radiated God to everyone around him. His face shone because of his encounter with the Living God and no one could deny he had been talking to the Lord. An important aspect of these verses is the fact that Moses took off his veil when he went to talk to the Lord, which we will talk about in a little bit, so remember that.

Now my face never actually shines after I pray like Moses' face did, but after my quiet times of solitude and prayer I really feel renewed and recharged. Do you? I don't think I've ever knelt down to meet my Savior and afterwards said, "Man that was time wasted," or "Oh, I feel like less of a child of God now."

Anytime, even if I didn't feel the presence of the Lord or felt like He had withdrawn himself from me, like Hezekiah felt in 2 Chronicles 32:31, I always felt revitalized.

At first I felt discouraged by not "feeling" His presence, but eventually this temporary despondency forced me to reevaluate my heart and I ended up pursuing the Lord's presence even more in prayer. Each time, I somehow knew that the Holy Spirit of God was molding me and working in my life to reflect His glory.

I said earlier that prayer is faith in action. As we'll continue to see, faith really is defined by our actions and choices throughout our lives and is not an abstract and intangible concept.

"Now faith is the assurance of things hoped for, the conviction of things not seen." –Hebrews 11:1.

"For we walk by faith, not by sight—" –2 Corinthians 5:7.

When we humble ourselves and go to God in prayer we are displaying our ultimate faith in Him because there is no tangible person in front of us. We are walking, metaphorically on our knees, by faith that God will perform the work in us that He promised us: to make us perfect as Christ is perfect.

There are many aspects of prayer that I do not believe we can ever fully comprehend in this existence because we are not God (praise Him for that!) and His ways are not like our ways. But comprehension is not the point; complete commitment to Jesus is. That being said, I do know one thing. The many facets of prayer all encompass the single goal of becoming more like Christ.

Prayer enables us to escape the distractions and confusions of this fallen world and traitorous flesh and allows us to be overcome with the love of the Holy Spirit. Only then can we reflect His love and glory to all. Without a saturated prayer life there is no power in our light to shine because He is the Light Source. The true purpose of prayer is to keep us continually *seeking* and *relying* upon communion with the Lord no matter what. Prayer is not centered on coming to God *with* requests, but on coming to God—with our lives.

The Influence of Prayer

*"Mind how you pray. Make real business of it.
Let it never be a dead formality."* –Charles Spurgeon [6]

There are two sides to a lack of faith in prayer that sever a child of God from the Vine and render them as fruitless as a fig tree: *questioning the sovereign grace of God* and *the doubt that prayer changes anything.*

Can you imagine Mary Magdalene, at the foot of Christ's cross, telling Jesus, "I still don't think you can cleanse me of my sin," as she watched the Savior suffer for all of humanity? Of course not! Were she to say that she would be belittling the suffering and saving grace of Jesus Christ. So why, sometimes, do we allow our sin to prevent us from approaching our Father in prayer?

For most of us, the misunderstanding about the sovereignty and grace of the Lord prevents ashamed and embarrassed followers of Christ from talking to the Father. They detach themselves from the rest of God's children and God Himself. I really wince at the mere thought of this, especially because it is quite common among Christians everywhere. Remember what Proverbs 28:13 says:

"He who conceals his transgressions will not prosper, but he who confesses and forsakes them will find compassion."

Too many Christians, myself included when I let down those I love, isolate themselves and hinder the Lord's healing hands to work in their lives. They turn away from Christ and His grace. They don't look at it that way when it happens, but that is what they are doing.

The underlying depth of this dilemma is far more serious than anyone realizes. The moment an individual does not seek His presence because they feel too sinful or wretched they are belittling the cross of Jesus Christ and disregarding, intentionally or unintentionally, His sacrifice. In addition, by doing so, they place God's supremacy beneath their own sin.

This situation is like that of a child who is in trouble but does not go to his parents about it because he doesn't think his parents can do anything to help or solve the problem. In essence, the child believes the situation is more powerful than his parents. The Lord is our Heavenly Parent. The moment we place God's authority or power beneath anything, sin or otherwise, is the moment that we question His very existence as God. Nothing is above God. The Lord is powerless before no one and no thing!

"...for *God is greater than our heart and knows all things.*" −1 John 3:20b (emphasis added).

He knows your heart, your struggles and your sin and desperately wants to draw you to Himself to love you and help you, even if it hurts. We do not have to clean ourselves up to come before the Lord because we have no ability to clean ourselves up at all! We can't do it! Only He can make us pure as freshly fallen snow.

Remember how Moses took off his veil when he went before the Lord in prayer? That is exactly what we are called to do. Rip off the mask that we show to the world, those closest to us and even, at times, ourselves and be brutally honest with God. Only then can we be emptied of our sin and filled with His righteousness. Every follower feels small and unclean before a Holy God but that should never deter us from seeking His presence because within His arms, and *only* within His arms, can we find mercy and redemption!

This fact continues into our prayers to God. If we pray to the Lord what we think He wants to hear and are not presenting our honest-everything, we are being false before Him who knows all things. David and the Psalms are a beautiful representation of unbridled honesty and holding yourself relentlessly accountable to the Lord. David bore everything to the Lord, even in euphoria, depression or white-hot fury.

There is no fooling the King of kings. So the only person you end up fooling is yourself. If we do not open up to God and truly place ourselves before His healing hands then we can never harvest the entirety of His blessings. Remember, Christ said that we must first, "Ask, and then you will receive." C.S. Lewis echoes this by instructing us to "lay before Him what is in us, not what ought to be in us." [7]

The second side of a lack of faith is just as detrimental to the follower: the disbelief that our prayers won't actually be answered. Just as detrimental and yet even more destructive. More destructive? Yes.

The disbelief of what we pray for is the silent killer to a life of faith:

"And Jesus answered saying to them, 'Have faith in God. Truly I say to you, whoever says to this mountain, 'Be taken up and cast into the sea, and does not doubt in his heart, but believes that what he says is going to happen, it will be granted him." –Mark 11:23.

Do you know what the core source of fruitlessness for the life of a believer is? It is the modern religion of our age: *skepticism*. When you pray, do you truly, with all of your soul, with all of your might, *know* that God is going to grant it to you? Now you may not know how or when, in fact you most likely won't, but do you believe He will move in your life because of your prayer, as He promised?

Too many individuals who I have come across and talked with in our modern society equate faith with naiveté. They could not be more wrong. Do you know why that mountain will move? It's not because you believe the mountain will move. It moves because you believe in Jesus, in His power and loving intervention. That mountain moves because of your faith in Christ, not because of your faith that since you want the mountain to move it will.

Prayers are always answered. Does this mean trouble or suffering will not come your way? No. It means that the Father always answers your prayers, just usually not in a way that we can see or understand—because He is God! Will God keep you in His hands if you ask him? Of course. But occasionally the answer to prayer is a time of tribulation that forces you to completely rely upon His grace and strength, which ultimately saves you from a separation from Christ and keeps you intimately within His grasp.

Even more perplexing is the fact that sometimes the answer to your prayer is *silence*. This is perhaps the most baffling aspect of prayer to me. God truly withdraws Himself from our presence sometimes (see Hezekiah again). He does this to test us and strengthen our faith in Him because faith is not about a feeling or proof, it's about choosing to follow no matter what. We'll get into the intricacies of faith a little later.

A fickle faith in the power and sovereignty of God cripples the Spirit's ability to produce any and all fruit. Does this limit God in moving through us? No, it limits us in our response to and obeying of the Holy Spirit's movements within our hearts and lives. Remember who the Vine is? Why do we deny our Redeemer's greatest gift and sacrifice with the worst insult imaginable: a lack of faith?

"Therefore I say to you, all things for which you pray and ask, believe that you have received them, and they will be granted you." –Mark 11:24

The Reality of Prayer

"Prayer is learned behavior. Nobody is born an expert at it. No one ever masters prayer." –John Ortberg, The Life You've Always Wanted [8]

I really don't enjoy algebra; mainly because I don't really comprehend it. Formulaic equations and complex graphing doesn't come naturally to me at all. God gave me more of an artistic mind and so math and I have always had an understanding: I don't like it and it doesn't like me.

But I know that algebra, like anything that does not come natural to me, will only become a tool I can use effectively if I practice it. In fact, any unnatural task must be practiced (repetition, repetition, repetition) to become less foreign and more *second-nature*.

The spiritual disciplines, especially prayer, are the same. What do you think about prayer? Do you think the longer you are a Christian the more naturally prayer will come to you and can be checked off on the "Christian Things I Have Mastered" list? The apostles of the Lord Jesus, who were in the daily presence of the greatest pray-er to walk the earth, still needed help with it and asked Him, "Lord, teach us to pray." How much more do you think we have to learn and grow in prayer throughout our lives?

An attitude of "checking off" prayer as one of the "been there, accomplished that" aspects of Christianity will unfortunately leave us lacking an alive relationship with God. More so it will rob us of the blessings and communion with God linked with prayer. Prayer is not something we conquer and then move on to the next spiritual discipline or fruit of the spirit. Relationships hinge upon communication and the amount of time you spend with someone.

It is quite true that whatever you deem as most important in life is the thing that you spend the most time doing. Unfortunately for me, apparently the most important thing in my life is either viewing college athletics or playing video games (and if I ever had the guts to admit it, watching so much television has got to stop as well).

We must sacrifice our time, we are called by His Word to do that, and *devote* not just time, but our very lives to Christ. That doesn't mean an hour and a half every Sunday, it means every moment of our lives. "Impossible." Yes, without God it is and *that's the point*.

Without surrendering everything before the God of creation in humility and love we lose focus on His glory and end up only exalting our own dim and tainted version of it when we pray—if we pray. Why is prayer a "learned behavior" that "no one masters" or "is born an expert" at? The answer is right in front of you. In fact, the answer is you/us; we are who we are—fallen, flesh.

Remember what we discovered in chapter one? Anything that involves the spiritual or holy will never be natural to us, because we are fleshly and sinners by nature! Sinners saved by grace and a new creation *in Christ*, never forget it! But we are children susceptible to sin nonetheless.

And it really is true that too many followers of Christ feel that the moment they give their lives to the Lord all the susceptibilities they have to sin should or will just vanish, at least I did, and that all the spiritual lifelines we have at our disposal (worship, prayer, mercy, patience, etc.) should all become as natural as breathing. Ha!

He has made us a new creation through His Spirit. We have not made ourselves a new creation in the flesh. Therefore we must work at becoming spiritually-centered as a *second nature*.

"Prayer does not happen automatically. My hunch is that of all spiritual disciplines, prayer is the one that people feel most guilty about. Somehow it seems that if we really love God prayer should flow out of us without effort or discipline…Like any other demanding activity, prayer requires a certain level of preparation." –John Ortberg [9]

Since prayer is so foreign to us we must approach it as we would a musical instrument we would like to play but have never touched. The first thing is practice. You do not become a virtuoso by simply picking up a violin and bow. No, you must spend hours upon days upon years of your life devoted to the practice of developing that skill. Prayer is similar. Without actually engaging in prayer you will never come to a greater growth in prayer. It is going to take a *conscious decision* and deliberate effort, like memorizing the strings or chord scales on a violin.

Secondly, pace yourself. "There is a principle of progression in the spiritual life. We do not take occasional joggers and put them in a marathon. If prayer is not a fixed habit with you, instead of starting with hours of prayer, single out a few moments and put all your energy into them." – Richard Foster. Be honest about your level and current customs regarding prayer. You'll only be attempting the impossible on your own if you don't. Also, stay focused upon God and not what you are performing. Remember:

"With man it is impossible, but with God all things are possible" – Matthew 19:26.

Lastly, we can't get discouraged! Our daily life is so hectic that any quiet solitude is going to take a little preparation to produce. And it will take an even longer time in that quiet solitude to clear our hearts and minds for the Lord. Just be patient and understanding. Wait on the Lord. Even if you can't focus on Him during prayer, wait on the Lord:

"Be still and know that I am God" –Psalm 46:10a.

Just let all those other loud distractions dissipate. Nothing outshines the Light of Christ. Believe me, all the hazy thoughts and disturbances will fade or be cleared by His radiance.

And eventually prayer will become second nature and produce sweet, sweet symphonic melodies to the Lord and everyone around us.

Prayer is not a Christian hobby or an out-dated tradition. *Prayer is the heart of Christianity.* The purpose, power and reality of prayer in the life of a *follower* of Jesus are essential components to *actually* following Him! You are called to prayer. Throughout your entire life the Father's voice is calling you to Him, to pray. Every moment of every day He is beckoning you. If you quiet your heart right now, clear your mind and wait—you will feel the tug. You will feel the call of God to seek His face in prayer. Do you feel it deep in your heart? Prayer is our sustenance in this dark and fleshly world! Prayer heals us like nothing else.

To love the Lord your God with everything is impossible on your own without a vital and vivacious communion with God! And it's even harder to love your neighbor as yourself without hearing Christ tell you how much He loves you—and them.

Application:

Pray. Sometimes it is as simple as that, but oh so difficult to make happen. Intentionally set aside five minutes today and give all of yourself to God in honest and focused communication with Him. For seven days deliberately set aside 5-10 minutes, to start, for prayer. (If you are accustomed to longer periods of time in prayer then set a time you feel is appropriate.)

In addition to this, remember to focus on maintaining a constant connection with Christ throughout the day through prayer (pray without ceasing). This does not mean close your eyes all day. It means keep your heart in constant conversation with the Lord. This will seem difficult and unnatural at first, but we must remember, such is the Christian life. Focus. With Him all is possible.

Also, try to imagine yourself actually talking to a person. If you need to, try and picture the face of Christ or the person of Christ in your mind's eye as standing in front of you or sitting beside you. You are much more likely to ask with confidence and belief if you are talking to Someone, than when you think you are just speaking into thin air.

And prayer is you talking to Someone: the Lord.

Also, remember to believe in God and that you will receive what you are asking for in His name, even if you don't know how. Stay focused on Him and do not doubt His power or majesty. There is no such thing as an incorrect or wrong prayer when you speak to Him in reverence and faith. Prayer is just opening your heart and life to Jesus.

Transformation is just a prayer away.

Prayer:

Dear Holy Father, thank You for the eternal life that we have in knowing You, the only true God, and Jesus Christ, our Savior, whom You have sent. Thank You for Your mercy and redeeming love. Thank You that You love us just as we are and that You welcome us into Your arms always. As Your Son asked You, Father, we also ask You to "keep" us so that we may be one with You. Help us to come to You just as we are. Help us to keep in constant communication with You so that the Holy Spirit You have blessed us with will continually overflow, with Your love and wisdom, into our hearts, minds and soul—and guide our lives. May we never take for granted the gift of coming into Your presence! May we never disregard the cross of our Lord Jesus Christ! May we forever be in prayer with You our God and Father! Amen.

Chapter Three
"For My Eyes Have Seen the King": Worship

> *"I can safely say, on the authority of all that is revealed in the Word of God, that any man or woman on this earth who is bored and turned off by worship is not ready for heaven."* [10]
> —A.W. TOZER

> *"There is a way of ordering our mental life on more than one level at once. On one level we may be thinking, discussing, seeing, calculating, and meeting all the demands of external affairs. But deep within, behind the scenes, at a profounder level, we may also be in prayer and adoration, song and worship and a gentle receptiveness to divine breathings."* [11]
> —THOMAS KELLY

If a stranger came up to you and asked you what worship is, what would you say? Would you tell them that worship was what you do at church before the sermon? Would you, could you, could any of us for that matter, tell them anything? Do you even ever really think about worshipping God?

Many people have a lot of opinions on what worship is and means today. The unfortunate thing is that many of them exclude the most important thing about worship: God. They focus so much on what worship has to be (the actions involved) and thus extract the movement and power of the Holy Spirit from those very actions. They've turned worship into their business instead of the business of adoring and revering the Father.

So, what does worship mean to you?

With all of the misunderstanding regarding worship, do we as children of God even truly comprehend what worship is or how to genuinely worship in the first place?

"Worship must be in spirit and in truth!...The stark, tragic fact is that the efforts of many people to worship are unacceptable to God. Without an infusion of the Holy Spirit there can be no true worship. This is serious. It is hard for me to rest peacefully at night knowing that millions of cultured, religious people are merely carrying on church traditions and religious customs and they are not actually reaching God at all." –A. W. Tozer, *Whatever Happened to Worship?* [12]

I strongly believe that true worship is the missing *heartbeat* of many a believer's fading lifeline with God. The most terrifying aspect about modern "worship" is that many Christians have mistakenly removed the Lord Jesus from worship through stimulating activities and intriguing speeches, without even realizing it! It's like we're trying to bake a cake without yeast and then, after sticking it in the oven for awhile and taking it out, we ask, "Why didn't it rise? I stuck it in the oven. The heat's supposed to make it rise."

An oven can't make a cake rise unless yeast is infused throughout the entire cake. An oven can definitely burn a cake to a crisp (which I have learned the hard way many times, much to the chagrin of my wife), no matter the contents. Unless the inside of that cake is right and prepared when it enters that oven, nothing will happen. Worshipping God is very similar.

Music, singing and actions in and of themselves will not raise our hearts and voices up to God in worship. Only when the Holy Spirit of God is in and throughout our words—throughout our very heart in all that we do, can our lives be offered up to the Lord in worship. If not then our songs and actions will only get burnt, instead of rising up to the Lord as an offering.

Many times we fail to comprehend that worshipping the Father is not at all about what we do, but what the state of our hearts, minds and souls are in at that moment. No matter how much I shout at the top of my lungs or raise my hands in the air, if I have not prepared my heart to sing real praise to God, if I'm not really thinking about God while I sing the word "praise," then they are just meaningless notes and words on page or screen.

Perhaps even more terrifying than this is the ever increasing notion that worship is only done on a Sunday before a sermon. In our modern Christianity, adoring and revering God have been confined to half an hour a week in a pew, if even then. Apparently, much of Christianity today definitely seems to be under the false impression that we are not meant to worship the Lord in *all* that we *do*. That's like saying that exercise is only something you do when another person provides you with the motivation and time to workout.

We exercise because fitness is vital to our body's survival and well-being, not when it is appropriate, convenient or scheduled. Can you imagine what state all of us would be in if we only exercised when we could all gather together and make it a scheduled event? Worshipping the Lord God is as crucial to your soul's survival and prosperity as exercise is to your body's health.

The misconception that worship is limited to a church building or a block of time for one day a week is as crippling to our metaphorical hearts before the Lord as not exercising is to our actual hearts. In the end, both hearts will stop beating.

I think the underlying motivation for relegating worship to a specific time during the week is that instead of making time to worship God every day, we tend to only worship Him when it is convenient for us. This horrible reality reveals to us the most telling aspect as to why many individuals don't really have their own personal definition of what worship is: because they don't give it much *thought, time* or *priority*.

Worship is why we're here. We were given life to praise and glorify God. We are here to worship Him at all times and with every fiber of our being, not just when it's convenient. Many people will say that it is impossible to be on your knees and bowing to God during every moment of your life. And they are right…in one sense. And wrong in another.

If they mean that you can't live your life on your knees and head down at all times then yes, they're right. But if they mean that you can't worship God apart from being on your knees and keeping your head down then they are wrong. Obviously it is impossible to be physically on your knees and expressing an outward action of worship to the Lord all the time. However, a physical action is just that, an outward expression of what is moving within your heart.

I can wrap my arms around a million people, but if I don't care about that person—am I really hugging them? Showing a sign of affection is more than just wrapping my arms around someone. It is the movements in my heart for them that lead to me showing affection. And those movements deep inside each of us are the ultimate indicator of whether or not we are really hugging someone.

Why? Because it is out of our hearts that we hug someone. Our hands and arms are just the visible signs of our affection. What's in your heart is just as important in worship as in physical affection because worship is our spiritual affection—our spiritual hug—to Christ. Hugging God is more than wrapping your arms around Him, it's the desire to hug, love, revere and be close to Him that constitutes worship.

And the best part is that God desires to hug, love and be close to us too! He's waiting on us to come and give Him the spiritual hug of our adoration and reverence. He is calling us to worship Him always. No matter what we may be doing or accomplishing, we must be in a state of "prayer and adoration, song and worship and a gentle receptiveness to divine breathings" to genuinely glorify the Lord Jesus. If you really want to worship God then you will, no matter what you're doing; when you do it or how you do it.

The Bible tells us we "must worship the Father in spirit and truth," so there are certain things, like sinning, that can never be true worship. But "in spirit and truth" is never defined as any specific activity or process. Let's look back real quick to the question at the beginning of the chapter. If a stranger came up to you and asked you what worship is, what would you say?

Would you answer what worship means according to Scripture or what it means specifically to you? Which do you think will give the stranger the answer they're really looking for from you?

I agree with A.W. Tozer that there are three fundamental aspects of worship: *mental, spiritual and emotional worship*. I would like to do more than just identify what the three aspects are though. Let's take an in-depth look into just what these three aspects entail in the life of a believer in Christ and maybe we'll all see how every follower of Christ must be continually and completely engaged in these aspects of worship throughout their daily walk to adequately honor and glorify their God.

Let us worship in the temple of God

"Do you not know that you are a temple of God and that the Spirit of God dwells in you?" –1 Corinthians 3:16.

What do people do in a temple of God? They worship! That's why they're there. We, His children, His church, are the temple of God. Every moment of every day we are called to worship the Lord. Not just to revitalize and empower us, but to bow and give praise in the Presence of the Father in *His* temple, in us.

All three aspects of worship are essential and key components to how you will *act* and *react* to everyday circumstances. These components all work to do one thing: prepare a place for the Lord inside your heart. And if we take a look at the importance of our hearts in worship, we can all see that without a humble and Spirit-filled heart, worship is impossible.

Mental: The way the Word speaks of "knowing" the truth of the Lord is a kind of understanding that you grasp with all of your being (your metaphorical heart). *Spiritual*: Where does the Holy Spirit of God dwell in each of us? Our heart. *Emotional*: How do we feel and encounter the Living God in our lives? How does He speak to us? He moves *in, throughout and speaks to*—our heart.

That being said, if "the mouth speaks out of that which fills the heart." –Matthew 12:34b, we can all see why, if the Spirit of God fills your heart completely, every word you speak and every breath you take will be worship to the Lord. All of our heart must truly be His in order for us to genuinely be His temple.

MENTAL: "THOSE WHO WORSHIP HIM MUST WORSHIP IN SPIRIT AND *TRUTH*" –JOHN 4:24B.

The mental aspect of worship is not thinking or pondering some abstract, theological concept, as many people believe it to be. In fact, it is not even really cerebral at all. The mental side of worship is an understanding, but it does not involve your head. Worshipping the Lord mentally is to know with all your heart, mind, soul and strength the divine nature and majesty of God – everything He is and everything that we are not. It's not about comprehension, it's about adoration.

This aspect of worship is perhaps the most overlooked component of authentic worship. To really know the truth of God and His splendor is an intense and amazing gift that we dismiss on a regular basis because we don't really notice it. It's a lot like appreciating being healthy when you're not sick.

When you catch a cold or are sick with the flu you have a completely different appreciation and fondness for being healthy than when nothing's wrong. Yet, after you get over your illness and are healthy again the thought doesn't even cross your mind. You take your wellbeing for granted. We all do this. We get so distracted with things that demand our attention that health is not an issue to us—until we get sick again.

The mental side of worship plays a similar role in our lives. I can't tell you how many times I'll be sitting at my computer or reading my Bible and I'll read John 3:16 or come across a scribbled note reading "How great is our God?" and I don't give it a second thought—until the beauty and majesty of the Lord demands my attention, like when I'm suffering or experience His hand on my life or the life of someone else I love.

I'm not going to lie, it's really hard to appreciate the Lord for all He is if we don't try to appreciate His divine glory, *which is the point of worship!* We make *thinking about God a priority*! But all too often thinking about and loving God for His holiness is not a priority for us. Instead we usually focus on what the day will hold for us and the things we must accomplish without ever truly dwelling upon the intimate knowledge we have of our Holy Father. Slow and steady may win the race, but fast and frantic is the pace.

Why do we push God out of our thoughts, hearts and ultimately our lives? Because God doesn't push and force Himself into our thoughts. He lets us live this life freely to either choose Him or deny Him. God has given us the responsibility of including Him in our lives. Remember, He has promised us in James 4:8a that if we draw near to Him, He will draw near to us. His Voice is calling you to draw close to Him, not just on Sundays but on every single day; He wants your devotion on a daily basis (nights as well, but I'm sure you know what I mean):

> "Is it not a beautiful thing for a businessman to enter his office on Monday morning with an inner call to worship: 'The Lord is in my office—let all the world be silent before Him.' If you cannot worship the Lord in the midst of your responsibilities on Monday, it is not very likely that you were worshiping on Sunday!" –*A.W. Tozer* [13]

So what is it about us that makes keeping worship a priority in our day so difficult? There are a number of reasons, but the two most prevalent ones are:

1. We have a tendency to place worshipping the Lord into a calendar, as we discussed earlier. We schedule it for a specific instance in the day, week, month or year that we have "time" for, instead of allowing the true worship of Christ our Savior to define and edify our lives; and,

2. An intimate and genuine encounter with the presence of Almighty God is man's greatest joy or man's worst fear. We shall look at this more in the Emotional aspect of real worship.

> SPIRITUAL: "THOSE WHO WORSHIP HIM MUST WORSHIP
> IN *SPIRIT* AND TRUTH" –JOHN 4:24B

It's no accident that the spiritual element of worship is at the center of the three aspects: Mental, Spiritual, Emotional. The Spirit of God is and must be at the center of our worship for it to ever be worship. The Spirit of God is the center magnet that draws the mental and emotional aspects of worship to itself.

Any disciple who is overflowing with the Spirit of God is echoing throughout all of creation the sweet melodies of authentic worship. Their very life is worship because the Holy Spirit of God is alive and in the midst of their heart and actions. However, without the intercession of the Holy Spirit dwelling in your life, nothing, no matter what you do, will ever be worship. With His Spirit everything you do is worship.

> "In the same way the Spirit also helps our weakness; for we do not know how to pray as we should, but *the Spirit Himself intercedes for us with groanings too deep for words*; and He who searches the hearts knows what the mind of the Spirit is, because He intercedes for the saints according to the will of God." –Romans 8:26-27 [emphasis added].

Is that not one of the most beautiful and moving phrases in all of Scripture?

"The Spirit Himself intercedes for us with groanings too deep for words."

I've experienced this verse firsthand. You probably have too, when you are so overwhelmed with the Lord, when your eyes tear up and your lips quiver in quiet contemplation or celebration of what Jesus is to you. In those moments your mouth couldn't form words to describe your requests or feelings if someone paid you. It's like trying to whistle with a mouth full of crackers; it's just not going to happen.

Sometimes when the human heart is so overwhelmed with love for Christ we can't really talk to God about it. That is when the Holy Spirit of God, who dwells most actively in our metaphorical hearts, steps in and whispers Hallelujah's to our Father on our behalf.

Sadly though, many believers are wary of taking hold of this aspect of worship because it removes from them the authority and power behind worship. "Amen!" I say to that! It's not about us! We all have a tendency to pick and choose what parts we get to do and what parts we have authority over and then what parts we should turn over to God—instead of giving everything to Him.

Wherever you look in Scripture, where there is the undeniable presence and work of the Holy Spirit there is true worship no matter the circumstance (the whole book of Acts testifies to this, especially Acts 7: 54-60: The stoning and death of Stephen, which personifies keeping your mind fixed upon glorifying the Lord no matter what).

Why can we not worship genuinely without the Holy Spirit? Because after the fall of Adam and Eve, man's relationship and connection with God has been eternally severed. We can not encounter God or be graced with His glory unless we continually invite Him into our life and into our hearts. Such is the basis of spiritual worship.

"For to us God revealed them through the Spirit; for the Spirit searches all things, even the depths of God...Even so the thoughts of God no one knows except the Spirit of God." −1 Corinthians 2:10.

Worship does not originate with us, it moves through us. The Holy Spirit of God is constantly testifying to us the holiness and majesty of God. Everything, all of creation, worships the Lord. Submitting to the Holy Spirit's divinity and sovereignty is the only chance we have of worshipping our Father. This also means preparing our hearts and surroundings as suitable places for the presence of the Holy Spirit, which by no means is an easy thing to do.

Many times I have been quite content to stay grumpy on my way to church because of traffic lights, which seem to be involved in a conspiracy to keep me from arriving to church on time, or when my beloved, fantastic wife is running just a little bit late (it helps, guys, to keep repeating how wonderful she is to yourself when she makes you ten minutes late to anything, or else you'll be the one in trouble in the end for getting upset about it in the first place).

It is extremely hard to push all that out of our hearts to make room for the Lord, but just because it's difficult does not mean it's not necessary. It is. If you, a friend, or a loved one doesn't want to be around you when you're cranky, what makes you think the Holy Spirit does? And though the Holy Spirit of God will never leave you nor forsake you, if your heart and temperament are in a continuous state of animosity and grumpiness then you will make it very difficult on yourself to respond to the gentle whispers of the Spirit.

If you're not in the "mood" for worship, what makes you think your "mood" will magically alter on its own? Only you, through the assistance of God's grace, can change your heart because only you are the one who is responsible for the state that you are in.

We, as believers, sometimes appear to be so focused on the procedure of "worshiping" that we remove or do not even invite the Holy Spirit into His own operation. We can never forget that it is the Spirit of God who whispers into our hearts, minds and souls the passageways of how to please the Father through worship.

EMOTIONAL: "THOSE WHO *WORSHIP* HIM MUST WORSHIP IN SPIRIT AND TRUTH" –JOHN 4:24B.

The emotional aspect of worshiping God is not just one more sentiment to tack onto your list of feelings. It's beyond a feeling. Encountering the Living Lord is an intense experience of a man or woman before the very face of their God.

> "Some people talk as if meeting the gaze of absolute goodness would be fun. They need to think again. They are still only playing with religion. Goodness [God] is either the great safety or the great danger—according to the way you react to it. And we have reacted the wrong way."
> –C.S. Lewis, *Mere Christianity* [14]

To be overcome by the glory and majesty of God is an all-together overwhelming and surreal experience. This encounter is debilitating and uplifting, damning and redeeming, joyous and heartbreaking, peaceful and frightening, produces love and shame.

In short, it is the created meeting the Creator; the unclean in the presence of unbearable Holiness; children in the arms of their Father. Genuine worship of God is not a "feeling" at all. I can't tell you how frustrated I get when I catch myself saying the sentence, "I didn't really feel anything like worship today." As if the only way to know if you've worshipped the Lord is through a fuzzy feeling or a divine glow throughout the world around you (which would probably terrify me to my core and make me think I was radioactive).

A feeling does not define worship. Worship is to truly *appreciate* the wonders of God despite feelings or circumstances. One of the best examples of genuine, emotional worship is giving thanks to the Lord no matter what, because when you truly appreciate the wonders of God you can't help but thank Him for everything in your life, for even having a life in the first place! Now this may at first seem like yet another impossible aspect of worship and Christianity as a whole, but rest assured that it is not.

The moment you genuinely begin valuing the Lord and His majesty is when all of the sweet echoes and reverberations of Him resonate around you and through you all the louder. For instance, a beautiful sunrise shines upon you with more than just warmth or light, but bathes you in the power of God. Music becomes the distant symphonies of the angels' chorus in heaven. And all of creation permeates with the nearly-tangible presence of the Lord Jesus Christ.

And as you appreciate who Christ is you then invite the Spirit of God to come and enable you to experience true humanity. Worshiping the Lord Jesus means experiencing the depths and entire spectrum of human sensation no matter your situation. Christ Himself is the perfect example of this truth. He eagerly made Himself aware of every single joy, pain and love that crossed His path. Not once did He numb Himself to the suffering of others or to the richness that just being alive another day truly is. How?

Jesus was intimately connected in constant worship and communion with the Father. With that being said we can now see that worship is so much more than actions or an ideological or theological concept. Worship is a state of mind, of living, a communion with and reliance upon the Holy Spirit; an *approach* toward all that you encounter and experience, especially God. The emotional side of worshiping God is to love, adore and vividly sense all that the Lord is. You don't feel worship with your emotions, but with your hungry soul.

Can any of us honestly say that our daily lives and walks with Christ (which are in reality the same thing, but for some reason we like to separate them) are characterized by an attitude and predisposition to love and adore God in all we say, do or think? I can't. But one day, we all *can*. One glorious day, we all *will*. So how about we all start preparing now!

Most of us will only love and adore God when we have good reason to because we have received blessings, gifts or feel like God is taking care of us. That's not worship. It can't be. Worship means loving God when you don't feel like you should. Worship means adoring God when you're angry at Him, like David and Job did.

Real worship defines your life, instead of you defining it.

We have been given life in order to worship the Lord. We are meant to live this life, in Christ, in a continual state of loving adoration and awe-filled reverence before the Lord mentally, spiritually and emotionally. A lack of real worship eventually hollows you out and leaves you lost. True worship edifies your daily life.

Authentic worship is essential to loving the Lord our God with all our heart, soul, mind and strength. So, next time someone asks you what worship means to you—let them know.

Application:

For the next week, try to be in a continual state of mind of worshiping the Lord. When you wake up, thank the Lord for the day and ask for His help to keep you focused on Him. Pray that His Spirit would continually flow in and out of your heart throughout the day.

Also, remember to thank Him for everything that comes into your life that day. Be it as simple as a particularly tasty breakfast or even a beautiful sunrise. Because when your mind is fixed upon Him throughout your day, you will begin to hear echoes of His glory and majesty reverberate throughout all of nature, art and life.

If you have never had an intense and overwhelming encounter with the Lord, I encourage you to seek the company of Almighty God today. It doesn't take some complex formula, just humble yourself and seek His face. Devote yourself to a quiet time of solitude with Him. Just focus on entering the presence of the Lord.

Set your mind, spirit and heart on really worshiping God at every moment and experience for the next week.

Prayer:

Dear Holy Father, we thank You for Your Son and our Savior Jesus Christ. We ask that You would draw us near to You through the blood and sacrifice of Christ. Let us never forget the love You have for us. May we constantly keep our minds, spirits and hearts fixed upon Your face and Your will. Let all that we do be done in worship and let all that we are be an offering unto You. We love You and adore You, Father. Fill us with Your Holy Spirit and let us please You not with our words or actions, but with our lives. All of this we ask in the precious name of Jesus and for His sake always. Amen.

Chapter Four

Man Can't Live on Bread Alone: The Word of God

"The goal is not for us to get through the Scriptures. The goal is to get the Scriptures through us." [15]
—John Ortberg

"Your word I have treasured in my heart, that I may not sin against You…I will meditate on Your precepts and regard Your ways. I shall delight in Your statutes; I shall not forget your word."
—Psalm 119: ב Beth

The air is so hot that each breath you take feels like you're inhaling fire. The sun has scorched the ground around you so much that the sandals on your feet are even too hot to walk on. Even worse than the unbearable heat, the flesh-blasting wind mixed with sand and the sunburned skin that has begun to crack and ooze blisters is the fact that you haven't eaten or drank anything for forty days.

Can you picture it?

How weak you would be both physically and mentally? How weak you would even be spiritually? Because forty days in a desert wilderness without food, water or shelter is almost unbearable for a human being. Because forty days of a blazing sun cracks lips, burns skin and leaves the human body in such a state of physical debilitation that you scarcely have energy to open your eyes.

And yet, it is in this hour, this state of being, that the Lord Jesus Christ is brought into the most dangerous moment of His life. It is in this moment that Satan decides to tempt the Son of God:

"Jesus, full of the Holy Spirit, returned from the Jordan and was led around by the Spirit in the wilderness for forty days, being tempted by the devil. And He ate nothing during those days, and when they had ended, He became hungry.

And the devil said to Him, 'If You are the Son of God, tell this stone to become bread.'

And Jesus answered him, 'It is written, 'Man shall not live on bread alone'" –Luke 4:1-2.

The temptation of Jesus in the wilderness gives us the most stunning and clear model of how we can not only defend ourselves from spiritual attack and temptation to sin—but how to defeat it. His weapon of choice is an armament we all have in our repertoire: the Holy Word of God. The Messiah met every temptation with the truth found in Scripture. This monumental victory in Christ's life can not be overly stressed and must never be overlooked because we must realize how true of a temptation Christ faced in that frail hour.

Jesus is hungry, weary and in pain from forty days of fasting in the wilderness under a scorching sun and in the midst of blasting winds. Yet, this is why He went into the wilderness in the first place: to empty Himself and become vulnerable. But not just to temptation, but vulnerable to the power and guidance of Almighty God! We are all called to be so vulnerable (open) to the instruction of the Lord that when the Lord clears His throat we prepare ourselves to speak.

That is what fasting is all about: to empty ourselves of our dependence to the flesh and this world and to invite God to see that He, above all things, is our nourishment and our strength. And once we have placed Him as our only source for nourishment and strength, He *will* guide us. To truly become strong in Christ we must become weak in our "selves." We will go more in-depth later in this chapter about the three temptations Christ overcame using the Word as His protection but, not only did the Word nourish, and protect Christ in the wilderness, the Word of God transformed Him.

If someone were to ask you what the Holy Bible is, what would you say? Probably, the stock answer is, "well, it is the Word of God." While this answer is correct in a general and rather cold manner, I wonder if *our definition* of what the Bible is and the *reality* of what Scripture is—is the same. For instance, when you read your Bible, do you expect to meet the Living God in each verse? Every time you delve into the red letters, are you anticipating an encounter with Jesus the Christ?

If we really consider the Scriptures as the Living Word of God don't you think it is about time we start treating them that way? The term Living is not just something you toss around. The idea is that the messages and stories of the Old and New Testament are not only relevant and enlightening, but alive and overflowing with the very Living Spirit of God.

My personal experiences with reading the Bible have left me wondering what the true nature of this source of blessings should be in my heart and life. I fear I have looked at the Divine Scriptures with an eye fixated on history and information instead of HIS-story and the transformation of me. When followers of Christ open their Bibles they should prepare themselves for an encounter with the Living God; not a distant or data-giving encounter only, but a heart burning, mind baffling and soul shaking meeting with their Lord.

Do you consider the Word of God as alive and transforming in your life? Or do you only look at the thousands of pages as "a large book I really should read?" One sentence of Scripture that conforms us to the image of Jesus is as powerful as all sixty-six books combined. That is the very purpose of the Living Word: to become like Christ!

Have you ever contemplated the significance of Jesus Christ being the Living Word of God? He is Scripture wrapped up inside of a man from Nazareth. Our Savior is the Living Word of God. He lives! Therefore, any time you grace the pages of Holy Scripture (including even the territories of the tribes of Israel in Joshua) your fingers are grazing the pulsating veins of Jesus Christ, of the Living God.

Ever thought about the Bible that way? It brings a whole new dimension to *Bible Study*, doesn't it? We should really change it from Bible Study to *Christ Encounter*. The Word of God is not about information. It is not about the amount of verses we read, but the manner in which our hearts and lives change through encountering the Lord's will and message.

> "It is uniquely in the Bible that we encounter Jesus…Be open to the possibility that God is really speaking to you through His Word. Read the Bible with a readiness to surrender everything. Read it with a vulnerable heart. Read it wisely, but understand that reading for transformation is different from reading to find information or to prove a point. Resolve that you will be obedient to the Scriptures…To be filled with knowledge about the Bible but to be unwashed by it is worse than not knowing it at all."
> –John Ortberg [16]

I find it quite sad and ironic that spiritual transformation is usually the last thing on my mind when I read the Word of God, even though that is the whole purpose of following Christ: to become more like Him and less like me.

The Three Roles the Word of God Plays in Our Daily Lives

The Word of God is meant to play three, very crucial roles in our daily lives. Understanding these three truths of the Word is a necessity for any believer who wishes to follow their Savior wherever He may lead them, especially through this fallen and dark world. These truths are that the Word of God is our *nourishment*, the Word is our *security and sword* in this battlefield called the world and that the Living Word of God is here not only to inform us, but *transform* us.

THE WORD IS OUR NOURISHMENT:

"Your word is a lamp to my feet and a light to my path. I have sworn and I will confirm it, that I will keep your righteous ordinances.

> *I am exceedingly afflicted; revive me, O Lord, according to Your word...Sustain me according to Your word, that I may live; And do not let me be ashamed of my hope."*
> —Psalm 119:105-107, 116

As we saw earlier, when Christ in Matthew 4:4 quoted Deuteronomy 8:3 to fend off Satan, "Man does not live on bread alone, but on every word that proceeds out of the mouth of God," He meant it. When He said "I am the Living water," He meant it. I fear that our view concerning the role and purpose of Scripture has been tragically skewed. We have been under an intense illusion that something other than the Lord will satisfy and sustain us. Now most likely this is not an intentional thought or deliberate mistake taking place in our minds, but the idea that something else besides Christ can fulfill us is there nonetheless.

For example, look at the last installment's ideas of prayer being the "last resort." We seem to turn to the Lord only when we have exhausted our own limited abilities and resources to handle a problem or situation. What does this imply? This implies that we feel we are capable of handling and sustaining ourselves until there is nothing more *humanly* possible that we can do. Then *and only* then, after we can do no more, we turn to the Divine for guidance and support.

The great heartbreak of this line of thinking is that there is nothing in this life that enriches our lives and gives us "food." This world is a desert that stretches on far past the horizon with only scorched sand and slithering serpents to "nurture" us. A desert filled with mirages of lust, pride, wrath, greed, empty romance and self-centeredness that distract us unto the point of starvation and dehydration. When we drop to our knees in this life, this world, to feed our hunger and quench our thirst—all we are doing is scooping up sand into our mouths. Apart from God all that we try to consume in an attempt to fill our empty hearts is nothing but quicksand, which eventually sucks us down into the pit.

Enter Jesus Christ.

If we look at the account of the Samaritan woman in the gospel of John, we see that the Word of God is the only source of nourishment that lasts eternal. We see that Jesus alone gives life. Jesus alone is the living water in a dry and barren land we call the world. Jesus has asked the Samaritan woman for a drink when she asks Him why He is even talking to her since a Jew would become ceremonially unclean by drinking out of her cup.

"Jesus answered and said to her, 'If you knew the gift of God, and who it is who says to you, Give me a drink,' you would have asked Him, and He would have given you living water.'

She said to Him, 'Sir, You have nothing to draw with and the well is deep; where then do You get that living water?'...

Jesus answered and said to her, 'Everyone who drinks of this water will thirst again; but whoever drinks of the water that I will give him shall never thirst; but the water that I will give him will become in him a well of water springing up to eternal life." –John 4:10-14

Have you ever had a case of cottonmouth so bad that you could barely pry your tongue from off the roof of your mouth? Ever been so parched that the slightest drop of water in your mouth is like showering under Niagara Falls? There is a term I like to use for every time I feel the Word of God edifying me and guiding me: *refreshing*.

Have you ever gone days, weeks or months without opening up your Bible? Can you recall the first moment, after not reading Scripture for a long time, that you knew the Word was talking to your heart, overwhelming you, gripping you with a love so tight that you could not escape the power of each verse? Tasting the sweet sustaining Spirit of God is the same. Once you have had the taste of God's Holy Spirit in your life, nothing else will satisfy you. Nothing else can. I love the blunt and honest response of the Samaritan woman to Jesus.

"The woman said to Him, "Sir, give me this water, so I will not be thirsty nor come all the way here to draw." –John 4:15

To paraphrase a wiser man than I, "the day we associate the Word of God as being equally important and essential to our existence as eating, drinking and breathing are—is the day we get a little closer to understanding discipleship." The Word of God is our nourishment; the only nourishment that will never run dry.

Genuine Christianity, in its simplest and most basic form, is being completely unable to let go of the Savior no matter the circumstance or state of your heart. Because once you've felt His love, there is nothing else to satisfy you. There is simply nothing else except Jesus.

The Word is Our Security and Sword:

"Finally, be strong in the Lord and in the strength of His might. Put on the full armor of God, so that you will be able to stand firm against the schemes of the devil. For our struggle is not against flesh and blood, but against the rulers, against darkness, against the spiritual forces of wickedness in the heavenly places…and [take up] the sword of the Spirit, which is the word of God."
–Ephesians 6:10-13,17

This world, as C.S. Lewis stated, is "enemy occupied territory."[17] The realization and acknowledgement of this Scriptural truth must lead a follower to one conclusion: we are always at risk. Our faith is always in very real danger. We *will* be attacked. You *will* be attacked. Be it spiritually, intellectually, emotionally or even physically, your faith in Jesus Christ will be targeted.

As we all saw in the temptation of Christ in the wilderness, the assault upon our devotion to the Lord is a foregone conclusion for anyone who loves God. The Word of God is vital to our survival in the midst of an ongoing war. I do not use the term war lightly, but I *do* use it because I firmly believe that the fight for a person's soul is as nasty and serious a war as anyone will ever experience. And the world, the flesh and the devil are in a constant assault against the Holy Spirit within us. Stand firm in the faith! Arm yourself!

So how do you prepare for this unavoidable and imminent assault? Most of us ignore it or even worse, never acknowledge that there is a risk and dismiss it all together as an old and superstitious reverie. "That's just simply not a part of my life and walk." Ignoring an attack you know is coming is not absent-minded, it's just plain foolish (according to the Word of God). And the Bible is not too fond of fools. So how do we prepare for the battles to come? Well, follow the example of Christ in the wilderness! The Messiah used the Word of God to battle an attack upon His soul. Jesus didn't just sit there waiting for the devil to take off the gloves, He unleashed His sword and fought back.

The devil tempted Christ with three temptations that each of us face daily: *proof, power* and *protection*. Christ overcame these temptations by utilizing the strongest and largest weapon in His arsenal: The Word of God. Let us look at how Jesus conquered these three temptations.

THE TEMPTATION OF PROOF:

"And the devil said to Him, 'If you are the Son of God, tell this stone to become bread'" –LUKE 4:3

Now the devil is not the only one who tempts us with the trap of demanding proof. And a treacherous trap it is. You see, we really don't see asking for evidence as a trap at all because that's what we all want and desire: tangible proof. We all want to see, and hear, and smell, and taste and touch God. Because once we do, we will know with our senses that He is real.

And of course this is exactly how the devil, the world and the flesh want us to think. They want us to focus on the "burden of proof" because the only proof the flesh can find is physical proof. "God is spirit," as John 4:24 tells us and so to demand physical proof from a spiritual being is an exercise in futility and sets us up for disaster.

Not only this, but the flesh wants us to think that way because once we align our idea and relationship to God with an only-physical existence we do one very dangerous thing: become blind to the moving of the Holy Spirit within us. The day in which we so align ourselves to coming into the presence of God as an only physical feeling or physical experience is the day that we cripple the Holy Spirit's ability to help us grow and be with us. Why?

Because we won't be listening to the Spirit or opening our hearts to His whispers of guidance, love and edification. We will be looking for a giant, flashing, neon billboard. I know that I have looked for a billboard from the Lord on certain occasions that I needed guidance and I was so focused on searching for the billboard that I nearly abandoned seeking God all together. I was so dead-set on finding the "billboard" that I almost made the quest for the "billboard" my god and guide, instead of the invisible Lord Jesus.

You see, people will always ask for proof when it comes to believing in something, because they don't want to become vulnerable and open themselves up to the possibility of being hurt or mistaken. But as we'll see in a later chapter, the burden of proof, if used tyrannically in the life of a Christian, will squash the splendor of faith.

Now I'm not saying don't use good common sense or God's gift of reason to each of us when making decisions or believing in anything. Many individuals have followed false gods and been deceived under the horrible misuse of the word faith. God gave you a mind that can deduce fact from fiction and you should definitely use that gift. But never let God's gift of reason surpass God in your mind and life. We must keep God and not reason, or even the splendor of the mind, as our Lord.

So what is Christ's reply to these dastardly temptations and trials? He used the Word of God. In response to proof the Lord Jesus puts everything into perspective. "It is written, 'Man shall not live on bread alone.'"

THE TEMPTATION OF POWER:

And he [the devil] led Him up and showed Him all the kingdoms of the world in a moment of time. And the devil said to Him, 'I will give you all this domain and its glory; for it has been handed over to me, and I give it to whomever I wish. Therefore if You worship me, it shall all be Yours" –LUKE 4:6-7

The temptation of Power is a most wicked temptation indeed! How many men and women have fallen prey to this little morsel of might and influence while forfeiting their souls? The devil knows that this is perhaps, more than anything, what a fallen mankind craves most: power. How does he know this? Because this is the temptation the devil himself succumbed to, which is why Satan is so adept at using it on us.

Some individuals think money is the sin that most leads people astray, but I ask you, what does money get you? It gets you power. What has been the one aspect of history that has stayed true to all the rulers and kingdoms of the earth: Those without power crave to be powerful and those in power crave even more power.

Why is this temptation so debilitating? Well this is quite simple as well: to have power is to be god-like and ever since we were told we could "be like God" by the master of lies, we've always wanted to be a god. Basically it comes down to pride again. And that's why the devil tosses this temptation Christ's way.

Surely He'd fall for it. Adam did (in his own way). Eve did. Surely He will.

But He didn't. Why? It's a wonderful offer if you stop and look at it: be crowned the ruler of all kingdoms and dominions, be recognized as lord of creation; all of that with just one little requirement of worshiping the devil. So why did the devil's pitch fail?

Because Christ is the Lord of Creation; He doesn't need to be recognized as a god of heaven and earth because He is the God of heaven and earth! Bam! Christ doesn't desire more power because He is power personified. And within this truth is found the beauty of perfect power: He who has the power of the universe at His fingertips would rather be crowned with thorns and bend His knee in surrender to give that power away for free to those who would believe in Him, instead of exalt Himself and horde His power.

So how does Christ fend off this attack? "Jesus answered Him, 'It is written, you shall worship the Lord your God and serve Him only.'" I constantly marvel at how wonderful the Word of God is at putting things into some serious perspective. There is only one God and only one power in the universe: Jesus Christ. Yet, instead of serving Himself, Christ served the Father. For within the service of the one true God is found true power. And to serve God is to worship Him, as we discovered earlier. And when we worship the Lord through service we have the power and self-sacrificing love of Jesus at our fingertips so that we might help others to worship and serve Him as well.

The next time you feel the tug of temptation for power, remember that Christ's power is already inside your heart and alive in your life. Remember who is the King of kings and Lord of lords because within His loving, gracious and selfless arms the true power of God manifests itself to all of creation. The Word of God helps keep our allegiances in perspective and allows us to see the truth behind the lies, no matter who's telling them.

THE TEMPTATION OF PROTECTION:

And he [the devil] led Him to Jerusalem and had Him stand on the pinnacle of the temple, and said to Him, 'If you are the Son of God, throw Yourself down from here; for it is written, He will command

His angels concerning You to guard You, and, On their hands they will bear You up, so that You will not strike Your foot against a stone"
—Luke 4: 9-11

This temptation is very deeply-seated into each of us because this lie of the devil is based on a truth of God, which most lies are. There is not a single human being on the planet who does not yearn for security and peace; who does not wish to be protected by the Almighty Lord of Existence.

And this is not an all together evil desire, in fact, it is a wonderful thing to want to be safe in the arms of the Father. However this desire has been twisted and corrupted by many, many preachers, televangelists and people who call themselves Christians, not to mention demons and the devil.

There's no wonder the devil employed this trick against Christ; those who suffer or will experience suffering want to be exempted from pain by the hand of God. Who wouldn't? And Christ knew very well what was about to happen to Him. Christ knew what was on the horizon for the end of His life. And the devil knew it too; which is why the devil reminded Christ that He could, as the Son of God, call out to the angels at any time and they would catch Him.

I still, to this day, marvel at how much Jesus Christ must love us that He would put Himself willingly through so much pain and agony with the full knowledge that at any moment He could call upon the Army of Heaven to end His suffering. And on top of that, I marvel at just how much God must love us to turn His back on His Son and allow Christ to die a horrible death on the cross without lifting a finger. I just can't fathom that kind of love.

But I can definitely say Hallelujah. And thank you, Jesus.

So the devil, fully knowing what Christ would be asked to endure for the sake of mankind's salvation, reminds Christ of the way out of suffering in the Lord's weakened and already painful state.

"And Jesus answered him, 'It is said, 'You shall not put the Lord your God to the test.'"

The Word of God equips us to defeat pain and suffering by reminding us:

"Blessed be the God and Father of our Lord Jesus Christ, the Father of mercies and God of all comfort, who comforts us in all our affliction so that we will be able to comfort those who are in any affliction...for just as the sufferings of Christ are ours in abundance, so also our comfort is abundant through Christ" −2 Corinthians 1:3-5.

God's Word sends away the devil by the force of Christ's authority. Christ was at His weakest, physically, when He waged war with the devil in the wilderness. Yet, when Christ was weak, He was strong, as Paul tells us:

"And He has said to me, "My grace is sufficient for you, for power is perfected in weakness.' Most gladly, therefore, I will rather boast about my weaknesses, so that the power of Christ may dwell in me.

Therefore I am well content with weaknesses, with insults, with distresses, with persecutions, with difficulties, for Christ's sake; for when I am weak, then I am strong" –2 Corinthians 12:9-10.

The Word of the Father grants each of us His strength in times of weakness and starvation, testing and temptation and assault and attack. Because when we are weak in our own physical abilities we rely more upon the abilities of the Almighty, which are endless and unbeatable. We all must make it a point to depend upon the Spirit for our strength and solace all of the time and not our own limited faculties. One of the best ways to orientate yourself to depend completely on the Lord is to be fortified by His Word.

Now many people grow uncomfortable or begin to shift in their seats at the idea or mention of "spiritual warfare." I can understand this, believing in something you can not see is quite difficult to acknowledge, especially if it means that you might need to take things a little more seriously and take on a little more responsibility. Or in other words, *Welcome to the Christian life*! The Christian life *is* believing in what we can't see and taking a tremendous amount of responsibility for our actions, for our very lives.

Not acknowledging that you will be tempted and attacked is as harmful to you as not exercising or taking care of your body. Will it kill you instantly? Usually not. But over time you can handle less and less resistance, until you are trapped and helpless. Without using the tools at your disposal to not only defend your faith but encourage others into a relationship with Christ, you are becoming spiritually stagnant and treacherously sedentary.

We have been given a commission to spread the Word of Christ to all peoples. It's impossible to fluently and effectively use your sword if you've never taken it out of its scabbard before the battle.

You must know that the Word of God is your shield against flaming arrows of hate, doubt, disaster and sadness. Not only does the Lord save you when you first turn to Him, but Jesus Christ, the Living Word of God, continually offers you salvation throughout every moment of your life. Christ is our strength, security and sword. Praise God for His unfathomable love!

The Word is Our Transformation:

"All Scripture is inspired by God and profitable for teaching, for reproof, for correction, for training in righteousness; so that the man of God may be adequate, equipped for every good work." –2 Timothy 3:16-17

"If the Bible were to completely fulfill its mission, our minds would be so transformed—so filled with thoughts and feelings of truth, love, joy, and humility—that our lives would become one uninterrupted series of acts of grace and moral beauty. Every moment would be a miniature reflection of life in the kingdom of God." *–Pursuing Spiritual Transformation* [18]

Our goal is to love the Lord our God with everything we've got and to love our neighbors as ourselves. This principle can be summed up in another way: our goal is to passionately become more like Christ. This objective/purpose extends into everything we do. The Word of God is meant to change you into the likeness of Christ. How many of us look at it that way?

The Bible is here to transform us, not just inform us or give us new insights of inapplicable knowledge. Knowing is not enough. The Christian life is never about what you know, but the process of becoming more like Christ through *knowing Him*. This means we have to change and obey the Lord's Word. For me, Scripture has seldom been about transforming my life, mind and soul to His image. For a long time it was only about stockpiling Bible verses and quotes that I could use to debate or show off to everyone how smart and knowledgeable I was. I hang my head now at the mere thought of such reckless arrogance and blindness to the sweet mercy of Jesus.

A passionate and loving follower of Christ is to not just learn about Him but reflect Him. Every moment we spend in the memoirs of our Savior is a time in which we are meant to be attaching ourselves onto His heart, His Spirit. Reading the Bible is about loving your Father in Heaven by obeying His will. The Bible is not an instruction booklet designed to produce a shallow and empty "holiness." The Word of God is meant to live in each of our hearts throughout every moment of our day.

Jesus Christ is the Living Word of God. He dwells in each of our hearts through the glory and gift of the Holy Spirit. When we read Scripture the Holy Spirit gently (or not so gently at times) speaks to us as how to better follow our Lord and Savior by reproofing, correcting or training us. Our response to the call of the Holy Spirit is how we can tell if we are obedient or not.

I really do love the power behind the famous verse:

"And do not be conformed to this world, but be transformed by the renewing of your mind," Romans 12:2.

In it, the renewing of your mind is likened to being washed through and through with Scripture. I know that after a long day of stress and concerns that I am usually all too focused on fleshly, materialistic or temporary things. So because of this, I really feel like I'm caked in the mud of worldliness. I seriously need the giant bathtub of the Holy Word to wash out the mud that is caked all throughout the fibers of my thoughts and concerns.

Only can His eternal perspective and undeniable love for me, for you, wash out the world's screams and distractions. If we do not make the Lord our life in everything we do, the world can and will smother us with everything possible to distract and blind us from making Him just that: Lord.

The physical Bible, in all reality, is only ink on paper. Yet the message that these pages contain is the very life of Almighty God. It is the love song of a Savior willing to surrender everything for the ones He loves. It is the cry of desperate people so in love and yearning for the Lord that their very lives are poured out for His glory. It is the call to enter into the kingdom of God—today:

"The time is fulfilled, and the kingdom of God is at hand; repent and believe in the gospel." −Mark 1:15

The Word of God is not something you read to place a check mark on your "Spiritual Things I Have to Do Today" list. Scripture is to be viewed as a vivid encounter with a Living and passionately involved God. We should approach the Bible in a manner of expectation: we expect to be talked to, moved through and empowered by the Living God through His written Word. We should all prepare our hearts for the presence of Jesus, the Living Word, whenever our fingers grace the pages of the Word of God.

"My soul languishes for Your salvation; I wait for Your word." −Psalm 119:81

Application:

Encounter the Living God through His written Word. Every day this week set aside five to fifteen minutes (the time is not important here) to absorb a single verse (or chapter) out of the Bible. Just as Christ did, you usually must encounter the Lord in a place of solitude and serenity. It is vitally important that you spend this alone time with the Father, often called a quiet time, because it is usually only when we have separated ourselves from the distractions of this world and the business therein, that we open up our minds, hearts and souls to the whispers of His Word.

Approach this time alone with God as an intimate encounter with your Lord and Savior, not as a time to brush up on your Scriptural knowledge. Open your heart to the speaking of the Holy Spirit within you. Passionately pursue the presence of God and the sweet, sweet communion with Him through the letters and messages of the Holy Bible. Remember that you do not immerse yourself in the Scriptures for facts, but for a conversion of your mind, heart and soul to become more like Christ.

Humble yourself to meet the Lord and obey His commandments. Drink in the Living Word of God as the refreshing fountain it truly is.

Prayer:

Dear Holy Father, we thank You for Your written word. We thank You for the privilege we have to come close to You through the gift of the Scriptures. Thank You for blessing us with an opportunity to know Your heart and to encounter Your transforming touch in the Bible. Thank You for Your son Jesus Christ, who is Your Living Word. Help us to rely solely on Christ for our fulfillment and nourishment, because He alone satisfies. Thank You for Your grace, which enables us to come to You—that we might be transformed into Your likeness and reflect You. Father send Your Holy Spirit to rain down on us, to fill us with the living water that will overflow out of us and equip us to perform Your miracles and good works. We love You, Lord. May all that we do be done in the Spirit and in love of You. Bless us, Father. May Your Word dwell in us and we in Your Word. In Jesus name always. Amen.

Chapter Five

Clinging to the Vine: Faith

"You arrive at enough certainty to be able to make your way, but it is making it in darkness. Don't expect faith to clear things up for you. It is trust, not certainty." [19]
—Flannery O'Connor

"'If you can do anything, take pity on us and help us!' And Jesus said to him, 'If You can? All things are possible to him who believes.' Immediately the boy's father cried out and said, 'I do believe; help my unbelief.'"
—The Gospel of Mark

On one hot summer day, a ten year old boy walked with his father to get a chocolate ice cream cone from the dessert stand that was just across the street from their house. The boy was so excited that throughout the entire walk from their house to the ice cream stand he skipped a few steps in front of his father.

As they approached the intersection to cross the street the little boy stopped and then fidgeted impatiently as he was forced to wait on the walk sign to appear so he could cross the street, like a good boy. The father, though, was still a couple of paces behind his son and just out of arm's reach.

Now just as the words "walk" appeared under the stop light the boy eagerly strode towards the crosswalk. But before he could step off of the sidewalk and onto the asphalt a bike messenger, who wasn't paying attention to where he was going, violently collided into the boy. They both tumbled like anchors to the hard concrete beneath them. All the boy could hear was a very low growling noise after the impact.

As the little boy tried to get up off of the pavement with his hands already bloodied and scraped he saw his father just standing there. His father's face was blank. The boy began to grow very frustrated.

"Why didn't you save me, Daddy?"

The father just stood there slightly trembling, staring at his son as the bike messenger kept saying, "I'm so sorry, please forgive me. I just wasn't looking ahead." But the boy didn't hear any of that. All he cared about was the fact that his father had not stopped the bike from hurting him.

"Why didn't you stop the bike messenger, Daddy!" the boy said glaring at his father. "Why didn't you save me?"

The burning tears began trickling down his face as the boy sat there just a couple of feet away from the intersection. All of a sudden a forceful wind slammed into the boy's cheek as the low growling noise became a deafening roar. As the boy turned his head towards the intersection he saw a very large, red bus no more than two feet from his face. The red bus had zoomed through the intersection and over the crosswalk he would have been walking on just moments earlier, if the bike had not hit him. The driver had run the red light and would have blindsided the young boy.

The boy then ran into the arms of his dad as the father's frozen stare had been replaced with a fear that only a parent can understand: they know their child has just escaped tragedy. The boy, with his face buried into his father's neck, simply said, "I'm sorry."

What would you have done were you the boy after the collision with the bike messenger? If I had been the father, for instance, would you find it difficult to trust me if I had allowed the bike to crash into you while I was just a few feet away? If you saw and knew that it was in my power to prevent you from being struck by the bike rider and yet I did nothing, I did not move a muscle or stand in the way of the collision, would you still have an unshakable trust in me?

Of course not. Why?

Well, you'd be hurting and frustrated from the fact that you could not understand why I would not want to keep you from harm. As your palms began to bleed and burn from the cuts, you'd begin to quickly doubt my judgment. As the stinging pain set in you would begin to doubt my desire for your well-being. And as the tears swelled up and your vision blurred, you might even start to doubt if I had even ever been there at all.

And then how would you feel about me when you felt the rushing wind of the red bus fly by your cheek? Would your perspective change? Would you begin to place your trust in me again? Would you begin to have a hope that I really cared about your good? Could you overcome the doubt that scarred your heart?

Such is faith in God.

Faith is perhaps the most used word in Christianity other than Christ. And yet, it is most likely the most misunderstood and most difficult thing for us to have in this lifetime—let alone comprehend. Many, many believers feel incompetent and hopeless when it comes to having an absolute and unshakeable faith in God. They truly feel empty inside when it comes to having a "real" faith. So why is this? Well, the answer is crystal clear: because of their doubt.

Doubt happens. It is as much a part of faith as believing is. Did he just say something blasphemous? No, not at all. Not knowing what tomorrow will bring or what is going to happen in your life is essential to placing your faith in God. Dare I say—doubt is essential to the existence of faith?

How can you say that, you ask? Well, it's kind of a necessity for faith, if you really think about it. To begin with, when I say doubt I do not mean disbelief. But rather, I am talking about uncertainty. Disbelief and faith obviously are opposites so that can't be what I'm talking about.

Certainty and *faith* can never co-exist. If you always have proof, you can never have a blind belief. In short, if you are always 100% certain in life then you are certainly unable to live a life of faith. It's the great double-edged sword: we long to be given *evidence* from a *hidden* God. We want the Spirit to manifest Himself to us in the physical world as we are still in the physical world. We want certainty over faith. But faith is all He has promised and given us *for a reason*.

We want, as people, to see, touch, hear, witness and fully grasp that which is neither physical nor comprehensible: God. We want "belief" to be on our terms and not His. We want to be the ones who are in control despite the knowledge we have that, even if we had control, we would probably just mess things up.

We want to have and live this life of Christ on our terms and not have to surrender to anything that involves uncertainty because in the face of vagueness we all too often find ourselves afraid. But it is total surrender to the Lord's guidance and strength in times of fear that makes us genuinely faithful! Surrender is the ultimate test of a believer because it involves giving up every aspect of our lives. The great battle between faith and proof will most likely never end in the minds of Christ's followers. In essence, this tug-of-war is the definition of humanity's struggles with an invisible and seemingly distant God.

So then why has God only provided us with so little proof and yet requires so much blind faith in Him?

Not knowing and still believing is the essence of faith

The reason the Lord places such a huge emphasis on faith is because when we take a leap of faith towards Him despite all that the natural and physical world may scream at us, when our senses and human reasoning shout at us that there is nothing to catch us and that there is no God, *is precisely the moment when* we begin to crucify ourselves to the things of the flesh and this world and cling to the spiritual and eternal, to God Himself.

This truth is a lot like the time when you first learn to swim. As your parents bring you into the freezing cold water with gigantically fake smiles, which I'm sure is what immediately tips the child off to the fact that something is up, all you can think about is bath time. Because in your bath you know that when you dropped the shampoo bottle into the water, it sank. The same with your wash cloth, glug, glug, glug, to the bottom of the tub. So as your parents try to convince you to let go of them and trust the floaties on your arm, you think they're crazy.

"What! Are you kidding me? You want me to let go of you?! Are you crazy?" During the summer between high school and college I worked as a lifeguard at the YMCA. And let me tell you, I saw a lot of children who thought that they were smarter than their parents while in the pool. They'd hang on to the edge and just shake their heads at their parents as they tried to show them how to swim and that a person can really float in water.

And it was in this moment that I realized how similar faith in God is to learning how to swim. The problem that these children had is that they wouldn't let go of the edge because simply put, they could hold onto the edge. The side of the pool was what they could feel and grasp onto. They were *safe* holding onto the edge.

But they were robbing themselves of the joy of letting go and diving into the water. They were not allowing themselves to put away all the limited knowledge they had about things sinking in water and just hope and trust that their parents were right. And that is exactly what every single child of God must do. Children of God must let go of whatever edge they're holding onto that's preventing them from putting their complete hope and trust, in fact their very life, into the outstretched hands of their Heavenly Father, who is trying to lead him into the waters of splendor.

When we surrender our limited knowledge and control of our life over to Christ is when we give the Lord Jesus the ability to lead and sustain us, to not only keep us afloat but move us into the pools of His glory. And we can do this! But before we can, we must acknowledge a very humbling human truth: everyone suffers from uncertainty or fear. It is in our fragile, fleshly nature. Just look at the Bible. Peter, Thomas (goodness, poor Thomas) and even Job, the champion of faith, suffered from momentary lapses in their "belief beyond certainty."

And even worse, many children of God lose heart because they feel that they are so wicked and weak to still be suffering from doubt. They feel as though faith is something that they can never have or even deserve to have because after all this time as a believer in Christ they still don't believe *beyond a shadow of a doubt*.

And that is precisely what doubt or disbelief will be in your life: a giant shadow. Disbelief is a shadow that clouds the light of the Lord's sovereignty and love for you. And that shadow tries to cover the bright, shining flame of faith. With that said, uncertainty is not disbelief. And not knowing should never lead a believer into a depressed state that keeps them from the Lord. Does it from time to time?

Yes. Why? Because a relationship with an Individual who seems to always be hiding from you, in your view at least, is really frustrating and can put your faith to the test. Another reason that a relationship with God can be so exasperating and tiresome to us is that we seldom see any logic behind His actions.

We can never seem to understand why God does what He does. "That's not what I would have done," we often say in our minds. And yet the irony of this is that He doesn't have to defend Himself. God is God and we are not. Does it bother us that God never needs to give us an explanation? It does me; to be completely honest. But more so it should act as a relief for every follower of Christ. If we are fallen and continually make mistakes, isn't it a good thing that we don't understand or quite agree with how God handles things? I mean honestly, wouldn't it scare you if God did exactly what you would do in every situation, all the time?

The thought frightens me, at least, I'll tell you that much.

So is disbelief dangerous and crippling? Yes. Disbelief is more crippling than any other sin or thought because it brings into question the very existence and divinity of the Father. But I say again, not knowing what will happen and not believing that God reigns are not the same. And without the unknown we could never experience the *beauty* and *power* of believing in what we do not see and what we can not know: which is called *faith*. We would never be able to believe in God without requiring proof.

The Two Components of True Faith

For the longest time I thought that faith was the ability to have an unflinching confidence in the Lord no matter what. That no matter what happened or what honest questions crept into my mind, if I had real faith, I would not be affected in the least bit nor would my feelings towards the Father change. In retrospect, my definition of faith was more so a definition of a machine relating to God than that of a man. My concept of faith was more like a puppet or a hypocritical Pharisee, instead of the examples of David, Job and Paul.

In his book, *Reaching for the Invisible God,* Philip Yancey discusses what the driving force behind an authentic and mountain-moving faith should be:

> "As I look back over the giants of faith, all had one thing in common: neither victory nor success but *passion*. An emphasis on spiritual technique may well lead us away from the passionate relationship that God values above all. More than a doctrinal system, more than a mystical experience, the Bible emphasizes a relationship with a Person, and personal relationships are never steady-state." [20]

A cold and distant adherence to laws and regulations is one of the things that Jesus Christ abhorred most. Nothing, in fact, infuriated our Lord more.

Why? I believe that the separation that takes place inside a man who rigidly and unemotionally follows godly duties or spiritual techniques not only tears man away from God, but it slowly paralyzes true faith, which *is* passionately loving God.

Jesus, more than any other figure in the Bible, realized the utter danger of such a method of thinking and believing (or in all truth not believing). When you instinctively or habitually follow a guideline, doctrine, or godly command, without involving God in and throughout it, you become a hollow shell of flesh. And like a hollow wooden puppet, our limbs may be moving but our heart is just not in what we're doing.

"Every man's way is right in his own eyes, but the Lord weighs the hearts" –Proverbs 21:2.

A true faith in Jesus Christ requires a blind and passionate confidence in Him despite being smack dab in the midst of disaster, catastrophe and the unknown. Christ is our rock, our cornerstone. Jesus is what we build every single aspect of our lives on, because He will not and can not be shaken! Hallelujah to that comfort! Our passionate love of Jesus can foster and sustain a faith that shakes the foundations of the earth, moves mountains into the sea and reflects the beauty of Christ's undying faith in the Father.

There are two sides to faith that every follower of Christ needs to understand and partake of daily: *trust* and *hope* (overcoming uncertainty).

> "I have served in the ministry thirty years, almost thirty-one. I have come to understand that there are two kinds of faith. One says if and the other says though. One says: 'If everything goes well, if my life is prosperous, if I'm happy, if no one I love dies, if I'm successful, then I will believe in God and say my prayers and go to the church and give what I can afford.' The other says, though: though the cause of evil prosper, though I sweat in Gethsemane, though I must drink my cup at Calvary—nevertheless, precisely then, I will trust the Lord who made me. So Job cries: 'Though He slay me, yet will I trust Him' (Job 13:15)." –*George Everett Ross* [21]

Which kind of faith do you have?

Trust: having confidence in God despite whatever comes your way

"And we know that in all things God works for the good of those who love him." –Romans 8:28

Far too many believers do not really take to heart what Romans 8:28 means in regard to their lives and fall prey to doubt when catastrophes strike. They think, "If 'we know that in all things God works for the good of those who love him,' then I should always expect good things to happen to me." No, not in the least little bit.

You can expect and be assured that God works in your life for your *ultimate* good in every situation, from the good to the bad. This does not mean however that God will prevent suffering and tragedy from befalling you. This means that He is at work even in, no, especially in, those times of pain and fear. In all situations the Lord Jesus is working for your ultimate good. He wants you to have an ultimate good, as Yancey further shares with us:

"I am learning that mature faith, which encompasses both simple faith and fidelity [utmost loyalty], works the opposite of paranoia. It reassembles all the events of life around trust in a loving God. When good things happen, I accept them as gifts from God, worthy of thanksgiving. When bad things happen, I do not take them as necessarily sent by God—I see evidence in the Bible to the contrary—and I find in them no reason to divorce God. Rather, I trust that God can use even those bad things for my benefit. That, at least, is the goal toward which I strive." [22]

Christ is undercutting every incident in your life so that it will benefit your walk with Him, a.k.a it will draw you closer to the side of Jesus:

A faithful person sees life from the perspective of trust, not fear. Bedrock [the deepest, most solid] faith allows me to believe that, despite the chaos of the present moment, God does reign; that regardless of how worthless I may feel, I truly matter to a God of love; that no pain lasts forever and no evil triumphs in the end. Faith sees even the darkest deed of all history, the death of God's Son, as a necessary prelude to the brightest." –Philip Yancey [23]

I love that Yancey contrasts loyalty with paranoia because they really are opposites in all regards. For instance, if fidelity is seeing all events in life in the light that everything occurs for your ultimate good, then paranoia *is* the opposite: everything is assembled around a certainty that everything is out to harm you.

Beyond all the events of history, I genuinely believe that it takes a truly devoted child of God to see the cross atop the hill of Calvary as the way to paradise, not paranoia. The suffering in Gethsemane and the crucifixion of Christ are the two greatest examples of unparalleled and unshakable trust in a reigning God and loving Father, despite the fact that everything was screaming the opposite.

First, let us look at the Garden of Gethsemane and the words of Christ:

> "And He (Jesus) withdrew from them (the apostles) about a stone's throw, and He knelt down and began to pray, saying, 'Father, if You are willing, remove this cup from Me; yet not My will, but Yours be done'"
> –*Luke 22:41-42.*

The Son of God knows what He is about to undergo. Jesus knows that they are going to beat Him mercilessly, humiliate Him, curse Him, murder Him and worse, profane the name of His Father. So Jesus asks that if it be at all possible, "remove this cup from Me." Now, no one in their right mind would wish to undergo this suffering and hardship on their own accord. And yet, Christ's following sentence shows us that His desire for God's will overpowers and overcomes His desire for Himself:

"Yet not My will, but Yours be done."

Do you know what kind of trust a person must have to say, "Despite the fact that I'm about to endure the worst horrors of mankind, I trust that you know what you're doing." In the end, Christ trusted that His Father did know what He was doing.

He knew that His Father would not allow Him to undergo anything at all, unless it would, in the end, result in the greater good for God and all of mankind. That is trust. That is confidence in the Lord despite all reasoning. Now I know what you're probably thinking, "Complete trust in God was possible for Christ because He was the perfect Son of God and I am not! So how do you expect me to be like that then, huh?" Good point. However, let us never overlook the fact that we are sons of God now through the cross of Christ! And that through His Holy Spirit we are called to be perfect—in faith and fidelity. The Holy Spirit empowers us to be like Christ!

So let us look back at the Hill of Cavalry, at the three crosses on Golgotha, for a little guidance as to just what kind of a person we can be and must be to trust in God. Allow me to add my own spin on George Everett Ross's idea of there being two kinds of faith: the *if* and *though* faiths. I believe there are two kinds of people in this world, two thieves on the cross *within our hearts*. The one who believed despite it all and the one who couldn't.

"One of the criminals who were hanged there was hurling abuse at Him, saying, 'Are You not the Christ? Save Yourself and us!" –Luke 23:39.

I have regrettably been this thief many times in my life. Always doubting the divinity of Jesus. Actually commanding God to prove He is who He says He is by manifesting His power and glory out of selfishness, all for my wishes. In reality, I was testing the Lord my God for proof of His existence and sovereignty.

This thief *must* be crucified within each of us.

"But the *other* answered, and rebuking him said, 'Do you not even fear God, since you are under the same sentence of condemnation? And we indeed are suffering justly, for we are receiving what we deserve for our deeds; but this man has done nothing wrong. And he was saying, 'Jesus, remember me when You come in Your kingdom!'"Luke 23:40-42.

The second thief, the believing thief history calls him, trusted in the Lord completely as he hung on a cross, as both of them hung on a cross, dying. He trusted as he watched the very Messiah, Savior and Son of God, do nothing to save Himself. And even more amazing, even more unbelievable, is that the second thief saw God the Father do nothing to save His only Begotten Son from that agony and death and *still* he trusted.

Why did he trust so adamantly in Christ without hesitation or reservation? Because his heart had felt the tender touch of the Savior. And when that happens, no one, the thief included, can ever let Him go. And it is that thief that must be remembered in our hearts every single day.

'Jesus, remember me,' cried the thief.

"And He [Jesus] said to him, 'Truly I say to you, today you shall be with Me in Paradise.'" –Luke 23:43

Jesus remembered the thief. He remembered the thief's trust for all eternity. Shouldn't we do the same?

Hope: believing in God while in the midst of fear's flames

"There is no fear in love, but perfect love drives out fear....
We love because He first loved us." –1 JOHN 4:18-19

Without Christ there is no hope. Hope is the one thing that a Christian always has despite the conditions or blinding terror of this world, the wretchedness of death and the barbaric attacks of the devil. What would we be without the hope of Jesus and the resurrection? Nothing. We would be lost, terribly, terribly lost.

In a moment of reflection on some notes that I had made about my life before coming to Christ, I came to realize an incredible insight into the nature of God's love: "the only difference between the unbelieving world and me is the grace of God. The thing I have, a Christian has, that they do not is His hope."

So why is fear so crippling? Why does the Bible urge us hundreds of times to not have fear in our hearts or lives? Because fear leads to disbelief. Where one is, the other has already been at work. Without the love of God, without the hope of His salvation, we *are* lost and have good reason to be afraid.

But we are never lost once we are in the arms of the Shepherd! We are found! Christ's hope fuels us in our moments of "walking in the valley of the shadow of death." In fact, the presence of God is never more easily discernable than in the valley of shadow. Never more potent is the unbearable force of His love then when we are in suffering or distress. Why?

Because His face is all that can shine in our darkest times, because He alone can deliver us, because the sun shines its brightest through the dark clouds of a raging storm. The power and illumination of hope glows best in the dark valley of the unknown. Only in the unknown and unforeseen can hope ever really take place, because all else would be certainty.

One of the best examples of this is Daniel's three friends. If you remember, God did not save Meshach, Shadrach and Abednego from the flames of the furnace—He saved them while they were in the *midst* of the flames. It is then that trust in the Lord is all we have. In reality trust in the Lord is all we ever have, but it is in times of bleakness that we realize it most I think. It is in the flames of the furnace that we fully grasp the truth that He is our only hope. God is forever our *only* source of constant hope and strength despite anything that comes our way.

If you do not have the security that the Lord desires your good in all things, then I fear that you might be living only a shell of the life that Christ has for you. To live in fear is to question the love that God has for you. When we do that we start to question our very salvation, which in turn leads to hopelessness. Too many people take the beloved verse of John 15:5 in an only negative context:

"I am the vine you are the branches, he who abides in Me and I in Him, he bears much fruit. For apart from Me you can do nothing."

Yes, it is true that apart from Christ we can do nothing. But if that is so, then the inverse of that is also true. Together with Christ we can do anything and everything. How tremendous of a promise, of a hope, is that? "I can do all things through Christ who strengthens me." Philippians 4:3.

Never lose hope. Hope is the very gift that the Lord Jesus Christ gave us through His loving sacrifice:

"Many of His disciples withdrew and were not walking with Him anymore. So Jesus said to the twelve, 'You do not want to go away also, do you?'

Simon Peter answered Him, 'Lord, to whom shall we go? You have words of eternal life. We have believed and have come to know that You are the Holy One of God.'" –John 6:66-69.

"Lord, to whom else shall we go?" the apostles asked the Lord Jesus. Allow me to paraphrase their question if I may. "Who else is there but you, Jesus? How can we ever leave Your presence, Lord? How can we ever let You go?" The answer: we can't. Once our eyes have met the gaze of Jesus, nothing else will do. Christ is what we have forever. Christ *is* hope.

Faith is the shining beauty of God within the darkness of human doubt.

Application:

Approach the next week with the feeling and notion that in whatever you encounter, you will trust God's love and sovereignty in your life. Let nothing plant a seed of doubt in your life. Try to approach every situation, good or bad, with an utter confidence that Christ is with you and at work in your life.

Remember that uncertainty is a part of faith, but it is only the necessary component of an empowered faith. Overcoming that uncertainty is what empowers our faith. And we can only overcome through Christ Jesus our Lord!

Though sickness, pain and trials may come your way, you will still trust in the Lord. In fact, it is because of those distresses that we grow to trust in Him more. The cross of our Lord and Savior has granted to us an eternal hope in the glory of His love and the wondrous resurrection to come. Nothing can overpower or darken the hope that we have in Jesus Christ.

Your faith is the one thing that will be attacked throughout this process because the devil is the last person who wants you to start living a trusting and hope-filled life. So—trust and hope all the more!

Try to keep a constant focus and realization that God is continually at work in your life and you are never alone. He is with you always! Always!

Prayer:

Dear Heavenly Father, we thank You for Your unending and never-failing love for us. Thank You for sending hope, Your son Christ Jesus, into our hearts, lives and souls. Thank You that no matter what may befall us, You are there. You are there, at work in our lives, in order to refine us through the fire of faith, resulting in the perfection of believing, trusting and hoping in You despite all that comes our way. We love You, Father God. May we never lose heart and may we continually attach ourselves onto Your Holy Spirit, which is always at work for our good within every moment of this life we surrender to You. Keep us Father. Keep us and never let us go. Amen!

PART THREE

Applying the Grace of God to Every Day Life

Chapter Six

Embracing Weakness for His Strength: Humility

> *"The more humble we are in ourselves, and the more subject we are to God, the more prudent we will be in all our affairs, and the more we will enjoy peace and quiet in our hearts."* [24]
> —Thomas a Kempis

> *"God's great holy joke about the messiah complex is this: Every human being who has ever lived has suffered from it—except one. And He was the Messiah."* [25]
> —John Ortberg

Award shows fascinate me. It's not the glamour, or the glitz, or the tears of joy or disappointment. But there is one thing that happens at an award show that mesmerizes me to my very core: the acceptance speech. Seriously, just watch an award show and really listen to what is being said when the victor walks up the always-too-steep steps and accepts their award. You'll never witness a more precise portrait of the wide spectrum of the human condition than at a podium with a trophy being given away.

You'll see tears, screams, smiles, and sometimes panic. But even more enthralling is what comes through the tears, screams, smiles, and panic: messages. I find that individuals speak what truly overflows out of their heart when they give an acceptance speech. And it is within this context that humility becomes so crystal clear.

For the individuals who genuinely appreciate the honor they have just received, for the individuals who make us smile and think, "now they really deserved that," are the ones who know they could not have done it on their own. They are the ones who know how blessed they have been, not with the award, but with the people in their life who have invested in them so that they could receive the award.

It is those speeches that bring the tear to the audience and make hearts quiver as much as lips. Authentic humility captivates me because being in the presence of humility is so rare, so precious. Humility is why award shows fascinate me. Well, and also the lack thereof at award shows is equally absorbing, but in a more shock and awe sense.

There is a particular part of Scripture that has always reminded me of the red carpet and stage of an acceptance speech. The verses are found in the New Testament, more specifically in the Gospel according to Luke. In the parable of the Pharisee and the publican, in Luke 18:9-14, the Lord Jesus paints a poignant picture about how important a humble spirit is when trying to live an abundant and fulfilling life in Christ's grace:

"Two men went up into the temple to pray, one a Pharisee and the other a tax collector. The Pharisee stood and was praying this to himself: 'God, I thank you that I am not like other people: swindlers, unjust, adulterers, or even like this tax collector.

'I fast twice a week; I pay tithes of all that I get.'

But the tax collector, standing some distance away, was even unwilling to lift up his eyes to heaven, but was beating his breast saying, 'God be merciful to me, the sinner!'

I tell you this man went to his house justified rather than the other; for everyone who exalts himself will be humbled, but he who humbles himself will be exalted."

Now I don't wish to deride this Scripture at all, but which person would you want to clap for at an awards show? The differences between the Pharisee and the tax collector may seem immediately clear, but there is one difference between them that oft goes overlooked. The main difference between the tax collector and the Pharisee is not just their attitudes or speeches, but more so how they *related* to God.

The Pharisee, first and foremost, compared himself to the man standing next to him, instead of focusing upon the Lord to whom he was praying! He was so caught up in who he was and was not, that he lost touch of who God was, is and ever will be: perfect and holy. The Pharisee also beseeched the Lord with the good works that he had done and lifted himself up before God so that God could see just how "righteous" and "moral" the Pharisee was. The Pharisee stood proudly before the Living God and then exalted himself so that the Lord might behold the "goodness" of the Pharisee.

So with all the comparisons to others around him, do you think the Pharisee ever really felt like he needed to be justified or forgiven? Do you think the Pharisee thought more highly of the righteousness of God—or of his own? Did the Pharisee ask God for righteousness and justification or did the Pharisee tell God about his own righteousness and justification?

Now if you contrast what the Pharisee did with how the tax collector related to the Lord, you will be able see the secret to grabbing hold of the righteousness and glory found in Christ's graciousness. The tax collector beseeched the Lord not with his good deeds, but rather pleaded with God for His mercy to rain down upon the tax collector. He could not even bring himself to lift his eyes towards the sky because of his reverence for the Lord and shame for his own actions before a pristine God. The tax collector did not tell the Father why he was righteous, but rather asked the Lord to be justified only by the mercy and unparalleled righteousness of God.

As the tax collector shows us, anytime we are confronted with the real image of ourselves through the eyesight of a perfect God, despair and shame inevitably follow (the tax collector pounded his chest in agony over his sin). The truth within that painful insight into our hearts is that we can never earn salvation or approval through any tool or lifelong devotion to improving our "morality;" but only through devotion to God (discussed in-depth later).

We will be eternally undeserving when it comes to righteousness. However the inverse of that realization is true as well. If we can never attain perfection or earn salvation on our own but only through God's grace, then we can never sin beyond the bounds of the persistent pursuit of God's reckless love and forgiveness. Hallelujah!

And in the end of the parable Christ says that God regarded the tax collector justified (righteous) and forgiven, not the Pharisee. Why? Well, the answer is in the last line of the parable. "For everyone who exalts himself will be humbled, but he who humbles himself will be exalted." Any person who tries to lift himself up before Almighty God has no chance but to be humbled because even our best efforts do not compare to the holiness and perfection that reside in the Lord. Therefore, to truly be exalted we must bow before the Holy of holies in recognition of His splendor and penitently ask that He might graciously bestow upon us a shimmer of His glory *through mercy*, not validation.

This is why God counted the tax collector as righteous: The tax collector knew he had no righteousness of his own no matter his merits or undertakings. The tax collector knew the only righteousness or justification he could ever have was what the Lord blessed him with in his life.

As we can all see, the only chance someone has to be exalted is by God because He alone is the Most High. No one can exalt you higher than God for your amazing deeds because no one and nothing is above our Lord. Therefore, to be exalted God must be the one lifting you up in praise.

"Humble yourselves in the presence of the Lord, and He will exalt you" –James 4:10.

But here's the beauty of the promise from the Lord: *He wants to lift you up*. Because the moment you humble yourself is the moment you open your heart to the mercy and power of God's grace. Only when you pour out all the pride and desire for control in your life will you ever be able to be filled with the unsurpassed riches of Christ's love and praise.

"Well done, good and faithful *servant*." –Matthew 25:23 (emphasis added).

I urge you to never look past the word servant in that verse because to receive any real appreciation and gratitude from God or man, you must humbly serve in all of your endeavors. Because when your heart is humbled and empowered with His Spirit you not only have the touch of God on your life, but you echo the life of Christ into the world around you; you touch them with God's glory, which is a life overflowing with humility.

How Can We Overflow with Humility?

So how can we look out for the slippery slope of pride in our daily routine? Well, let's look back at how the Pharisee fell into the trap. The real fault of the Pharisee that started him on the downward spiral of sinful pride is the same mistake we all so commonly make: finger pointing. The Pharisee pointed his finger at the tax collector and said, "Well, God, at least I'm not like this guy! How good of a person must I be, since I am so much above this lowly tax collector here?"

And this is where the sin of pride slides so easily into our daily lives because we don't *associate* pride with this common occurrence at all. But ironically, we can spot it in someone else's life if they are the ones doing the judging. Nine times out of ten the only time we recognize pride is when it is pointed away from ourselves and towards someone else.

And in reality there can be no true humility of spirit until you have pointed that bull's-eye of your finger off of someone else and straight onto your own heart. Because, as everyone knows, it is a lot easier to point the finger towards someone else's mistakes than to shine a little Light on our own faults.

But that's the difficulty of the fight between pride and humility: we don't like to admit we're wrong. We want to appear to be perfect and under control no matter how imperfect or distraught we really are. Case in point, how many of you distort your height when someone asks you how tall you are? How many of you give yourself a few less pounds on your driver's license? How many of you blame your tardiness on the weather, traffic lights or the most telling of our finger pointing judgment—on some other driver?

I mean, seriously, in the grand scheme of things, what do we really think it accomplishes to mislead individuals to think we're an inch or two taller than we are or five to ten pounds lighter? Or that we have arrived late because of anything other than our own procrastination? The answer is: nothing! But, it does make us feel like we are coming off "better" than we really are.

Another living proof of this is the tendency of men to refuse to admit that they are lost. "I know where we're going. We don't need to stop. Well we're lost because you're reading the map wrong!" The generalization that men really, really don't like to admit they're wrong is well, generally true. We will never admit we made a mistake unless there is "beyond a reasonable doubt" of proof that we are lost and then we will most likely blame it on the navigator sitting in the passenger seat. At least I have.

There are a thousand other questions that men face throughout the day that they try to deny involvement in whatsoever. "Who broke the lamp? Do you know where you're going because I think we've passed that house like, five times? Is that what you're really going to wear to the banquet tonight?" The list goes on for miles.

And since women are usually the ones asking these questions, everyone should know precisely what I'm talking about whether you are male or female. Although many women in my life have proved that men are not the only ones who don't like to admit they're wrong. For instance, "You mean Dad shrunk my favorite shirt in the washer, Mom?" or "So a squirrel made you swerve and jump onto the curb and that's why you got into the accident, not because you were doing your make-up in the rearview mirror, Dear?"

But of course *both* men and women don't like to admit they're wrong because both men and women are human. No one wants people to know that they have made a mistake or that they aren't perfect. We don't enjoy shame or transparent failure (actually failure in general: invisible or visible). And yet it is only when you admit that you make mistakes and that you aren't perfect, that you can be freed from the shackles of shame through the perfect love of Christ. And I say perfect because genuine love is not dependent upon a person's abilities or track record, but on the realization that they are a gift from God.

We must take an honest look at ourselves in the mirror

Usually before we'll admit that we're totally imperfect, we will compare someone else's mistakes or shame to our own. And isn't it disturbing that comparing our shortcomings to someone else's always makes you feel more superior than they are, and even at times, like you never really failed at all—since the spotlight is on their failures now?

In fact, it is an unfortunate reality that many people enjoy highlighting the failures of others because it makes them not feel so bad about their own failures in business, family, or even worse, their relationship with God. I find it very unnerving that an individual is usually much more open to feeling better about their walk with God only after they have seen someone else fail or come upon hardships with their relationship with God. How many times have we patted ourselves on the back after reading our Bible for the day and finding out someone else we know didn't?

To really have an authentic humility, which is a person who shows love and respect for others above themselves, we must look at who we are not and then at whom we can become through Him. We have to turn that little finger back onto ourselves and take a good long look in the mirror at the person staring back. And this can be a painful event because a lot of the time we don't like what we see.

I believe that one of the biggest epidemics infecting and debilitating modern Christianity is the oldest and darkest sin of them all: self-righteousness.

> "We have all, in our own way, been trying to take God's place ever since [Eden] [...] pride destroys our capacity to love [...] pride moves us to exclude instead of to embrace, pride moves us to bow down before a mirror rather than before God. Pride moves us to judge rather than to serve [...] pride is essentially comparative in nature." *—John Ortberg* [26]

Let me ask you, how many times have you gone to church and looked around for the individuals who were not there? How many times, deep down in your heart, did you raise yourself above them for going to church when they did not? How many times did you judge them and place them below your "level of righteousness" because of their absence?

I've done it. And that confession still makes me sick to my stomach. "Do not judge or else you will be judged. For how you measure—it will be measured unto you." It's scary sometimes to stop and think how much measuring will be done unto us because of how much we looked down upon someone else.

Ortberg hit the nail on the head. Pride is always a comparison. Do you know why? Because vanity always originates out of a fixed focus on ourselves; pride always begins with "I." That's why we tear down others: to build up ourselves. "Well, I may be doing this, but at least *I am not* like 'this person' who is doing this. I know what *I am doing* is wrong, but everyone else is doing it, so I am no worse, in fact *I am better* because I know that what I am doing is wrong." Or the even more devastating and dangerous statement: "*I am so good* because *I* read my Bible today and *I* prayed today and *I* helped that little old lady cross the street and preached the Word to that awfully hedonistic man and sinfully lecherous woman. *I am so filled with God's grace and humility today!*"

Now I do not mean to poke fun at (well, maybe a little) individuals who think like this (mainly because I have thought this way before), nor do I wish to demean genuine good deeds for others because "faith, if it has no works, is dead." –James 2:17. But the irony behind becoming proud of our humility is very amusing to me because the moment we become proud of our humility is when we lose it.

The reason the last statement is so dangerous is that God is not as concerned with what works you do as He is with your motivation for doing them.

"All the ways of a man are clean in his own sight, but the Lord weighs the motives" –Proverbs 16:2.

And "good" works done out of wrong motives devastate a man and woman's spiritual growth because there are two thoughts that have most often brought about every person's fall away from God: how wonderful they are or how wonderful they could become through their own deeds or knowledge.

Well, every person except one.

WE MUST CONSTANTLY LOOK TO JESUS CHRIST, BECAUSE CHRIST IS HUMILITY PERSONIFIED

The model of our Lord and Savior's *life* and *lessons* to us are the only examples of complete and honest humility in the life of a person who has ever walked the face of this earth. The baffling thing about Christ's flawless humility, at least to me, is that this humility co-existed in a perfect unity with the power and sovereignty possessed only by God, which is a power and omniscience that would make anyone's head swell to the size of a hot air balloon.

To understand God's unending and astonishing grace is to come to the realization that nothing, especially anything involving our spiritual acts of obedience to God, will ever be good enough. Only God is good. So to truly be good, we must be overflowing with God. Then whatever act we do while filled with His goodness and righteousness will for all eternity be a good deed.

Uniquely within that reality, the truth of our insufficiency, lies the incomprehensible beauty of grace. Because of the love He has for us despite our wretchedness and lack of merit, we are forgiven and made good, washed clean. And we are made spotless *only* through the filtered eyes of a loving Father looking at us through the broken body of His son. Only when we have come to acknowledge our need for righteousness, do we invite His righteousness into our hearts. But how do we acknowledge that need?

To begin with, if we truly look in the mirror we will then start presenting the real person inside of us to everyone, even the mirror. We will start shattering our self deception:

> "Losing our illusions is painful because illusions are the stuff we live by. The Spirit of God is the great unmasker of illusions, the great destroyer of icons and idols. God's love for us is so great that He does not permit us to harbor false images, no matter how attached we are to them. God strips those falsehoods from us no matter how naked it may make us, because it is better to live naked in truth than clothed in fantasy." *–Brennan Manning* [27]

How much do we continually maintain the white pristine paint that covers the real us? Who do we think we are fooling? If Jesus saw through the Pharisees, do we not think He sees every single fabric of us? During the Lord's last discourse to the Pharisees, scribes and Sadducees, He delivered a scintillating warning against the self-glorification that we have all sought after at one time or another, or the pride that we can secretly harbor deep down inside of us instead of surrendering it as a haven for God's Spirit.

"Woe to you, scribes and Pharisees, hypocrites! For you are like whitewashed tombs, which on the outside appear beautiful, but inside they are full of dead men's bones and all uncleanness. So you, too, outwardly appear righteous to men, but inwardly you are full of hypocrisy and lawlessness." –Matthew 23:25-28

So we must ask ourselves a question: are we, more often than not, the hypocrites or the truly righteous men of God? Are we serving man or God? I still wonder sometimes why we constantly place such an emphasis on the way that we *appear* to be, instead of being honest about the state of who we are around others? I ask myself this question day to day. I exaggerate successes or failures to seem important or esteemed. What do we call those?

"Oh, don't be silly, those are just little *white* lies." They're white all right, whitewashed. They hide the rottenness inside. And why do I try to elevate myself in the eyes of others? You guessed it: pride again; putting myself before God.

Christ says "Woe" for a reason. Every time I embellish my accomplishments, *especially* if it goes unnoticed, my ability to discern the quiet whisper of His guidance fades away while my illusions and lies set up camp. If we are to be washed by the Blood of the Lamb, we must come to accept the degree to which we will be unmasked for what we truly are; the degree to which we will be left bare and unprotected. Because only in our vulnerable nakedness will we be redressed in the pristine garments of God's grace and holiness.

If "pride is comparative in nature," as Ortberg stated, then so is humility; the only difference is that in one you are comparing yourself to others and in the other you are comparing yourself to God. Humility is not bashing yourself or berating yourself about how awful of a person you are. Humility is not even really concerning yourself with your own worth at all, but more so, concerning yourself with the surpassing worth of having the Lord Jesus and being able to help those around you.

An authentic component of humility is comparing yourself to God, because when you do that you realize just what He is: *God*. And in this process you are forced (by your own grasp of His glorious might and mercy) to enact in the other integral part of graceful humility: Genuine gratitude for the love of God.

We must never take for granted the grace of God

When an unbeliever finally comes to faith in Christ they invite Jesus into their hearts to be Lord and Savior of their life. This realization and admission that they are sinners who need to be saved by God's grace is an essential experience of every born-anew believer. But I often wonder if we continue to see ourselves as sinners saved by grace after our conversion and salvation. I have seen many "children" of God, myself included unfortunately, turn unbelievers away because of self-righteous behavior. This unfortunate event happens every day; Christians drive away people who are seeking Christ.

But why?

Because the believer has lost touch with the truth: they need a Savior and are totally dependent upon Christ for redemption. I, for one, lose touch with this fundamental, Scriptural truth all the time. That even after my redemption through Christ, I am still imperfect clay and only possess any righteousness when it originates from God. This is a hard thing to admit for anyone because admitting that we still require God's grace means that we still have a lot of work to do, which can be a rather daunting thought.

If we were to continually treat the lost in this way, as we are no different than they are except for the saving mercy of the Lord, perhaps more people would see Jesus within us. And for others to see Jesus Christ we must take hold of the humility available to us through God's grace! To do so we must again look at the Lord Jesus for guidance.

So how does Jesus provide us with the key to this problem? He gives His life as the example and solution to give all believers the mindset of meekness.

"Do not be called leaders; for One is your Leader, that is, Christ. But the greatest among you shall be your servant. Whoever exalts himself shall be humbled; and whoever humbles himself shall be exalted." —Matthew 23:10-12

The only times I have felt exalted by God was, of course, when I had served the Lord and those around me. That discovery led me to this truth: the only exaltation that lasts a lifetime is the sweet song of Christ's quiet and *unseen* standing ovations. Only the silent, unheard applause of Christ can sustain this life of grace.

When you humble yourself, you start to see the authentic glory of putting yourself last and Jesus first, which means you put serving others and helping others first. And when that happens, you will soon realize that it is much better for your soul to go unnoticed as the one who serves, than to search endlessly for the spotlight. By standing in the shadows of secret service to others you will be edifying them in the strength of the Lord.

And during the rough times when you need encouragement, when life's struggles overwhelm you, you won't just have your own hands to lift you up but a multitude of backs to help carry your burdens. Because those you build up in Christ will be the ones who are there when you fail, to return the love of the Lord back to you. And all those who you have built up in the love of Jesus will be strong enough through His mighty compassion to carry you through any trial.

Now I'm not saying hand out fake honors or insincere applause to people, but when you have the opportunity to praise someone *do it*! The great malevolence of pride is that we are quick to recognize our own achievements and much too slow to recognize the accomplishments of others.

And don't think that humility is about not accepting compliments and praise from others. Remember the awards show? False humility rejects honest praise while saying "it was all God" with their lips, but "it was really all me" with their hearts. Humility is not about turning back praise and tribute, but rather keeping all of it in perspective!

And within the sentence above is the true wonder of Jesus Christ. He had such wisdom and brilliance that truly knew no bounds, except in the fact that He cared more about others than His own wisdom and brilliance! Isn't that just amazingly bizarre! I'll never be able to comprehend such humility. For that is what authentic, Christ-like humility is; it's not *denying* your merit, but *donating* it all to others, instead, as Christ did.

There is no greater gift to the Lord and to those around you than to have a humble heart because life really is a true joy when you are in the presence of those who think more about others and God than they do of themselves. I find that it is especially difficult to focus on loving others as Jesus does, when you're consumed with thinking only about yourself.

"Blessed are the poor in spirit, for theirs is the kingdom of heaven."
–Matthew 5:3

And the winner is…

Application:

First and foremost, if you have not admitted your guilt and need for redemption before God, ask Him to cleanse your heart and fill you with His righteousness through the forgiving of your sins by the blood of Jesus Christ. This is a requirement for not only experiencing the redemptive and edifying power of God's beautiful grace, but in spending eternity with the Lord.

Secondly, keep yourself in a constant mindset that the Lord Jesus truly is the Holy, exalted King of kings. When you begin to feel the urge to proclaim your own achievements or point out what *you* did for another person, stop and inwardly tell yourself, "It's all for you, Jesus." That exercise has continually helped me to not lose the humility of God's grace when I was about to need it the most: the next time I failed.

Another way to stay humble in heart is to lift up the efforts of others to the Lord and to those around you in praising them. Now this may seem like a trap for giving them a big head, but remember that humility is not about our rejecting compliments and praise, but rather keeping all of it in perspective! The perspective of Christ's holiness, sovereignty and love.

Prayer:

Our Heavenly Father and God, we can never offer You enough gratitude and thanks for the mercy and redemption that is found in the overabundance of Your grace. Thank You, Father, for sending us Jesus, the flesh and bones representation of Your kindness and love towards us, and for Loving us so, so much. We ask to remain in a lowly state of mind, not debasing ourselves or thinking less of ourselves, but merely realizing all that You are and precisely what we are not. We love You, Father God. Let us never forget Your grace and holiness in every single moment of our lives. Let us love and not judge one another, lest we be judged. All this in Jesus' name. Amen.

Chapter Seven

To Each His Own: Forgiveness

"The parables of Jesus reveal a God who is consistently overgenerous with His forgiveness and grace...in Jesus' stories, divine forgiveness does not depend upon our repentance, or on our ability to love our enemies, or our doing heroic, virtuous deeds. God's forgiveness depends only on the love out of which He fashioned the human race." [28]
—Brennan Manning

"To be a Christian means to forgive the inexcusable, because God has forgiven the inexcusable in you." [29]
—C.S. Lewis

Do you believe in forgiveness? And I don't mean with your head, but with your heart and your soul.

This question is a very serious one in the scope of heaven and hell, *mediocrity* versus *spiritual growth*. When I ask if you believe in forgiveness I don't just mean on a purely intellectual basis. When I say believe, I mean by the way you live your life and the way you treat the people you interact with every day, especially the ones who sin against you.

Because that's what forgiveness really is; believing through action:

"If one is a Christian," I thought, "of course one believes in the forgiveness of sins. It goes without saying." But the people who compiled the Creed [Apostles'] apparently thought that this was a part of our belief, which we needed to be reminded of every time we went to church. And I have begun to see that, as far as I am concerned, they were right.

"To believe in the forgiveness of sins is not nearly so easy as I thought. Real belief in it is the sort of thing that very easily slips away if we don't keep on polishing it up." –C.S. Lewis, *The Weight of Glory* [30]

C. S. Lewis was absolutely correct when he made the statement that a real belief in forgiveness, which is a daily practice of forgiving others in our lives, can slip easily away from us, the way a musical or physical talent does if you're not constantly using it, if you're not constantly practicing it. And once our belief in forgiveness begins to fade we can be very quickly left with a hardened spirit towards others and the Lord, which results in the further development of an unforgiving heart.

An unforgiving attitude is viciously contagious and has the very real capacity to infect the whole of Christianity because it does not just stop with one person. That person spreads it to their friend at the slightest mistake or wrongdoing against them because their heart is not tender and is not ready to forgive.

And this epidemic can spread so horribly that it ultimately can result in an outbreak of self-righteous and calloused hearts. The terror of ice cold hearts and concrete souls is that not being able to forgive someone does not only divide earthly relationships, but it also creates a rift between the heavenly and spiritual ones as well. A *lifestyle* of not forgiving will result in an *eternity* of not being forgiven.

There is a parable that is particularly poignant and powerful when trying to discover how to live a life of forgiveness:

"For this reason the kingdom of heaven may be compared to a king who wished to settle accounts with his slaves. When he had begun to settle them, one who owed him ten thousand talents was brought to him.

But since he did not have the means to repay, his lord commanded him to be sold, along with his wife and children and all that he had, and repayment to be made. So the slave fell to the ground and prostrated himself before him, saying 'Have patience with me and I will repay you everything.'

And the lord of that slave felt compassion and released him and forgave him the debt" –Matthew 18: 23-27.

Wouldn't it be fantastic if the story ended there? Wouldn't we truly be encouraged and uplifted by this wonderful tale of repentance and mercy?

Yep, *but* the parable doesn't end there- for a reason.

"But the slave went out and found one of his fellow slaves who owed him a hundred denarii; and he seized him and began to choke him, saying, 'Pay back what you owe.'

So his fellow slave fell to the ground and began to plead with him, saying, 'Have patience with me and I will repay you.'

But he was unwilling and went and threw him in prison until he should pay back what was owed. So when his fellow slaves saw what had happened, they were deeply grieved and came and reported to their lord all that had happened.

Then summoning him, his lord said to him, 'You wicked slave, I forgave you all that debt because you pleaded with me. Should you not also have had mercy on your fellow slave, in the same way that I had mercy on you?'

And his lord, moved with anger, handed him over to the torturers until he should repay all that was owed him." –Matthew 18:28-34

Why couldn't the slave just forgive as he had been forgiven? Because despite the massive amounts of forgiveness that was shown the slave, he felt like he was entitled to more than the mere *freedom* of even being able to forgive others. The slave wanted what other slaves owed him.

In short, the slave forgot about the mercy that his lord had showed him the moment he received clemency. Doesn't this sound a lot like the trap of the believer after conversion from the previous chapter? We forget that we have been saved by His grace and His grace alone and in doing so we treat those around us like we have never done anything wrong and that everything they owe us or everything they do against us is unforgivable. We act so appalled and betrayed by their "sin" because we have lost track of our need for a Redeemer and are then unwilling to offer a helping hand to pick them up when they are down. Instead, we often berate them when they're down and need our forgiveness the most. Don't we?

So what does this parable tell us are the results of not believing in forgiveness and not leading a life of forgiving others? In the last verse, Christ points out the results of not forgiving:

"My heavenly Father will also do the same to you, if each of you does not forgive his brother from your heart" –Matthew 18:35.

An unforgiving heart incapacitates our ability to love. And by leaving us incapable of loving others, we run dangerously close to forcing God to treat us as we have treated others: unlovingly. One of the easiest ways to see that this is true is the fact that to forgive is to follow the example of God and to not forgive is to distance yourself from God's likeness, since God is love. When you distance yourself from God by harboring an unforgiving heart it results in moving away from the mercy and grace of God. Basically, you make it impossible to really love another person by turning your back on the forgiveness of God.

"Therefore be imitators of God, as beloved children; and walk in love, just as Christ also loved you and gave Himself up for us, an offering and a sacrifice to God as a fragrant aroma." –Ephesians 5:1-2.

The beauty of forgiveness is the fact that when you forgive someone who has harmed you, you sacrifice your own sense of vengeance and payback for the glory of God.

"Be kind to one another, tender-hearted, forgiving each other, just as God in Christ also has forgiven you." Ephesians 4:25.

And just as Christ sacrificed His very life to make Himself an offering for our sins because of the love He has for us, we must offer up our own desire for retribution to God out of the love we have for Him. Because the more we love the Lord Jesus, the more we will be able to forgive those who have wronged us.

"He who is forgiven little, loves little." –Luke 7:47b.

Love, which can best be described in the previous verse as loving an individual through acts of charity, is a two-way street. The more charitable you are to another person the more likely they are to show you charity in return. The less charitable you are, the less charity you will receive. Therefore it can be easily inferred that if you do not receive forgiveness from others, which is a true form of charity, then the only explanation to be found is that you are not forgiving to others as well. You reap what you sow.

The parable shows us that when we fail to forgive others, we begin to doubt and question the sovereignty and wisdom of God because we pay back evil with evil and remove the Lord's right to repay those who have harmed His children.

"Never pay back evil for evil to anyone. Respect what is right in the sight of all men. If possible, so far as it depends on you, be at peace with all men. Never take your own revenge, beloved, but leave room for the wrath of God, for it is written, 'Vengeance is Mine, I will repay,' says the Lord...Do not be overcome by evil, but overcome evil with good" –Romans 12:17-19, 21.

We thus end up trivializing the overwhelming amount of forgiveness that Christ showed us while we were sinners by not forgiving the one little sin that our neighbor has done to us. Look back at the parable found in Matthew.

"Then summoning him, his lord said to him, 'You wicked slave, I forgave you all that debt because you pleaded with me. Should you not also have had mercy on your fellow slave, in the same way that I had mercy on you?'

And his lord, moved with anger, handed him over to the torturers until he should repay all that was owed him."

How to utilize Christianity's under-used and life-changing weapon: forgiveness

You see, we are the same as that slave in nearly all aspects except one: we have the ability to choose to forgive the sins of our neighbors and not meet the same fate. But we must fully understand that this is a daily choice that we make, not a one time "sure, I'll forgive others." Because to live a life of forgiveness will take every single iota of your love in Christ and for Christ in order to continually forgive those who not only hurt you, but even slander and hurt the Lord Jesus by hurting you.

"When you were dead in your transgressions and the uncircumcision of your flesh, He made you alive together with Him, having forgiven us all our transgressions, having canceled out the certificate of debt consisting of decrees against us, which was hostile to us; and He has taken it out of the way, having nailed it to the cross." –Colossians 2:13-14.

As you will begin to see, many of the spiritual disciplines bleed into another since they will often require the same type of sacrifice and subsequent loyalty. For example, humility and forgiveness are completely intertwined like ivy around a tree trunk.

Why? Because since humility starts with thinking of yourself less and focusing more upon Christ's glory, when a child of God can do this they make it possible for the Holy Spirit to lead them. This responsiveness to the leading of the Lord allows us to not focus on ourselves when someone has hurt us.

Humility allows us to forgive others because we are less concerned with what we deserve and can then grant mercy to those who have hurt us, like the Father shows each of us in Christ.

TRUE FORGIVENESS BEGINS WITH ACKNOWLEDGING OUR FAULTS.

Do you ever lie awake at night engrossed in regret? Do you lay there, unable to close your eyes, wishing or pondering, "If only I had said something else…" or "Why did I have to treat them like that?" If you do, then you are already on the right track to a career in the forgiveness business but you need to do one thing first: forgive yourself. Since forgiving others starts with believing that the Lord has forgiven you, you must forgive yourself of your own sin. And that can *only happen* when you acknowledge that you've done something wrong, that you've sinned against your neighbors and your God.

This means, though, that we must first completely own up to our mistakes instead of trying to justify, rationalize or excuse our faults or sins. Our choices do not need to be excused, explained or examined for "motivation" as to why we sinned against the Lord; they need to be forgiven. It seems that society today will do anything and everything to escape having to admit that people have to be held responsible for their own errors or faults in life. For instance, how many times have you heard the argument, "It's not my fault, it's in my genes," or "My parents didn't do this, so that's why I'm like this," or "I have anger issues, so I can't be blamed for anything I do really."

Now I do not want to come across as insensitive at all, because I myself know many family members and loved ones who suffer from substance abuse, abusive parents and mental volatility. However, despite the fact that these hardships may be *involved* in their struggles and in the decisions that they make, their hardships are not what ultimately *make any decisions*.

Somewhere along the line of events that lead any of us to pursue a course of action *we had to make a choice*. At some point, we made the decision that led to our error, not someone else. Excuses go out the door because when it comes down to it, the problem was not our circumstance but our *choice*. Every single one of us is the only one who makes the choice to do whatever it is we do. We may have tendencies that make it difficult for us to make the right decision and not sin against the Lord, but only you make up your mind to pursue a course of action. So you can't blame circumstances for poor choices, because they didn't make them.

No one ever forces a person to choose what to do, hence it is only the person who is ever responsible for his or her actions and decisions! Now individuals may pressure people or try to convince people to take a course of action, but somewhere in the process the person had to either agree with the individual or disagree. They either make the choice to not compromise no matter what is being said or they end up deciding to compromise and fall into sin.

That is why God holds only you and me accountable for our own lives and actions at judgment and not the people around us:

"But because of your stubbornness and unrepentant heart you are storing up wrath for yourself in the day of wrath and revelation of the righteous judgment of God, *who will render to each person according to his deeds*" –Romans 2:5-6 (emphasis added).

So if we can only look at ourselves as the person responsible for our transgressions, do we really have a right to judge others for their mistakes, as Christ tells us in Matthew 7:1-5:

"Do not judge so that you will not be judged. For in the way you judge, you will be judged; and by your standard of measure, it will be measured to you.

Why do you look at the speck that is in your brother's eye, but do not notice the log that is in your own eye? Or how can you say to your brother; 'Let me take the speck out of your eye,' and behold, the log is in your own eye?

You hypocrite, first take the log out of your own eye, and then you will see clearly to take the speck out of your brother's eye."

Imagine you have a tiny eyelash trapped beneath your eyelid. Doesn't your entire world stop so you can try and fish out that tiny, minute eyelash? Even more so, doesn't your entire vision come to a halt because of the tiny object scratching at your cornea? No matter how much you rub at it or try to open your eye, you just can't see anything. Now imagine that an entire two-by-four or a giant log is trapped beneath your eyelid. Would you be able to see anything at all?

Wouldn't the log, which Christ used as a metaphor for our own sins, completely take up your entire line of sight, your entire vision? So, if we can't see with a tiny eyelash blurring our view, how much more blind are we to the people around us when we are overwhelmed with the wretchedness of our own sin as Romans 2:1-5 shows us:

"Therefore you have no excuse, everyone of you who passes judgment, for in that which you judge another, you condemn yourself; for you who judge practice the same things. And we know that the judgment of God rightly falls upon those who practice such things. But do you suppose this, O man, when you pass judgment on those who practice such things and do the same yourself, that you will escape the judgment of God?"

That is why we offer up our sins to the Lord for forgiveness, so that He may remove the log of iniquity from our own eye and apply to us the eye drops of His Light so that we might see clearly again—through His eyes.

FORGIVENESS IS NOT ABOUT FORGETTING, BUT PARDONING.

There is a common misconception throughout the entire known universe that forgiving an individual means you forget what they did to you. This may come as a shock to you, but that idea is not only absurd, it's completely unbiblical. Real forgiveness necessitates remembering the transgression in all its fury and then, despite the pain, despite the betrayal, staring it in the face and saying, "I forgive you."

"But I have always been told, 'Forgive and forget.'" Well, what about that idea?

Have you ever tried to consciously forget about something that's firmly in your mind? (Don't we all wish that good information remained in our minds so permanently like the times that people betray us or hurt us?) In the effort to eradicate the painful thought you only end up concentrating on it more than you would have, had you not tried to remove it in the first place, which then makes you even more upset and frustrated than before.

If you are ever going to really forgive someone or yourself for a transgression, you have to remember the sin to genuinely forgive it and experience mercy. Because if you forget the transgression they committed against you or belittle its importance, then you can never *really* forgive what they did. And more importantly, you can never grow closer to Christ and become more like Jesus through that missed opportunity to forgive because you didn't show them His mercy:

"Forgiving does not mean excusing. Many people seem to think it does. They think that if you ask them to forgive someone who has cheated or bullied them you are trying to make out that there was really no cheating or no bullying. But if that were so, there would be nothing to forgive. They keep on replying, 'But I tell you the man broke a most solemn promise.' Exactly: that is precisely what you have to forgive. (This doesn't mean that you must necessarily believe his next promise. It does mean that you must make every effort to kill every taste of resentment in your own heart—every wish to humiliate or hurt him or to pay him out.)" –C.S. Lewis, *The Weight of Glory* [31]

This is also true in regards to seeking forgiveness from the Lord. Because if you forget what you have done to the Lord that hurt Him, (and our sin does hurt God, which is a thought I don't think any of us really want to dwell on or even really acknowledge) how will you ever learn from your sin and turn from it? You can't. If you never remember what you did wrong, how will you not do the very same thing again?

We must ask for forgiveness for our sins, not try to remove them from our minds; or else we are removing the grace of God as well from our lives. Who would want to repeat the sin that has led them astray from their Lord?

In addition, if we forget the transgressions against us from another individual and do not forgive the wrongdoing against us, our heart remains hurt and the pain begins to fester. We have already let a transgression perpetrated against us become our own transgression against that person or the Lord through the anger and the sin of not forgiving them.

Lastly, forgiving others means not treating them badly after forgiving them. It almost sounds ridiculous to read the previous sentence out loud. "Of course it means not treating them badly after you forgive them, sheesh! Because if you're still treating them badly, then you've obviously not really forgiven them."

Bingo. You said it (or read it) yourself.

But how many of us, then, are really forgiving people? Does the way we treat them afterwards indicate that we've forgiven them or does it prove that we still have some work to do? Remember, forgiveness does not mean forgetting what an individual has done to you, but it does mean no longer holding it against them after forgiving them.

As you can see, a heart of not forgiving is a vicious cycle of bitterness and stubbornness that has no end. The unending circle can only be broken by the scarred hands of Christ.

LIVING A LIFE OF FORGIVENESS MEANS CHOOSING YOUR FRIENDS WISELY.

Another danger is that if we fail to recognize the mistakes of others we will ultimately follow in their footsteps.

"Do not associate with a man given to anger; Or go with a hot-tempered man, or you will *learn his ways and find a snare for yourself.*" –Proverbs 22:24-25 (emphasis added).

I also believe this verse has much to say about who you decide to surround yourself with in life and friendship. If you are consistently being wronged by the people whom you surround yourself with, then perhaps you shouldn't be surrounding yourself with those people.

"He who walks with wise men will be wise. But the companion of fools will suffer harm." –Proverbs 13: 20

If you are constantly inviting individuals into friendship who consistently hurt people and lead you and others into sin, then you are already bringing harm onto yourself. In fact, you are probably jeopardizing your own walk with the Lord by remaining around these individuals (since they will be harming you so much) because you will begin to harden your heart towards others and in doing so, harden your heart to Christ.

Forgiveness does not mean subjecting yourself to the same pain over and over and over again, it means forgiving them in your own heart. And sometimes it does mean leaving the company of the person who has hurt you and yet, not harboring ill-will towards them in your heart. Because if you leave the "company of fools" and wisely place yourself in the company of Christ's disciples, you'll soon find out that it is a lot easier to become an authentic disciple of Christ when surrounded by miniature reflections of Him.

"Iron sharpens iron, so one man sharpens another." –Proverbs 27:17.

Forgiveness truly is an act that is altogether crazy to human reasoning and altogether crucial to becoming more like Christ.

"I have a right to be angry when someone has hurt me. I am justified in my bitterness and pain." I have heard many people make this argument and to most ears it is a sound case. But to the ears of a follower of Christ, it sounds awfully distorted. Why? Because we have no rights any longer. Because we gave away all of our rights to this life and to selfishness and have placed them in the scarred palms of Christ when we gave Him our life. Believe me when I tell you that the only person you end up dragging down by holding something against your neighbor is yourself.

And God's willingness to forgive you is dragged down as well.

We must believe in forgiveness and then use it to not only reflect the beliefs and likeness of Christ to all who look upon us, but to embody the very grace and mercy that the Father has shown to us, to everyone.

Application:

When you feel yourself begin to harbor an ill-will towards someone, quickly pray for them.

What?!!

Start praying for them. Because I have found that when you are locked in a conversation with the Lord about a person, it is extremely hard to hold onto any anger you might have for them because you begin to see them and love them as God does: unconditionally.

Also, if you catch yourself judging someone else stop everything you're doing right then and there. Then, ask the Lord to help you fill your eyes with His vision of that individual and His vision of yourself through Christ. Because when God fills your vision with how He sees you despite the multitude of your sin, you begin to realize how little that individual has sinned against you and that because of the sheer amount of our transgressions we have no right to condemn anyone for theirs.

Sometimes the only application in our daily life in terms of forgiveness is to grit your teeth, swallow your pride and either to their face or in your heart say, "I forgive you." Because when you do, you become one step closer to reflecting Christ to that person, not only the person who sinned against you, but to the person who is staring back at you in the mirror.

Prayer:

Most gracious and loving Father God, we thank You so much for the mountains of infinite forgiveness You have bestowed upon us through the precious name and sacrifice of Jesus Christ our Lord! Lord may we never take for granted the forgiveness we have in You and You alone! May we constantly praise You for Your unfathomable love for us in Christ! Lord, help us to forgive those that sin against us, as You showed us how through forgiving us. Because, Father, we don't want to end up sinning against You or hurting You through our own selfishness of harboring anger and resentment. Help us to lift each other up despite all of our faults, so that we may lift up those who do not know You. May we, Your children, reflect Your mercy and saving grace to all who see us and may we show it to each other. In the precious and holy name of Jesus and for His sake always, Amen!

Chapter Eight
Taking Up the Cross of Christ: Devotion

"To experience the love of God in a true, and not an illusory form, is therefore to experience it as our surrender to His demand, our conformity to His desire: to experience it in the opposite way is, as it were, a solecism against the grammar of being." [32]
—C.S. Lewis

"Father, if You are willing, remove this cup from Me; yet not My will, but Yours be done."
—Jesus of Nazareth

What does devotion look like to you? If someone were to come up to you and ask you, "Judging by the way you live your life and what you pursue most with your time and abilities, what are you most devoted to right now?"—what would be your answer?

Usually, if this question results in any amount of serious contemplation, then the answer is most definitely not God. Which begs the question then, as a Christian, what are you devoted to if it is not Christ? And an even more troubling question is, as a Christian, why aren't you completely devoted to Christ?

"If you love Me keep My commandments, you will abide in My love; just as I have kept My Father's commandments and abide in His love. These things I have spoken to you so that My joy may be in you, and that your joy may be made full." –John 15:10-11.

Many people these days are definitely devoted in their life but instead of being devoted to Christ, they are devoted to using their skills for a cause. They are more devoted to "noble" causes than to the will or grace of God. And be it a noble cause, a political cause, a doctrinal cause or even an evangelical cause, if we are devoted to anything, *ANYTHING* above the Lord Jesus Christ, we are not surrendering to His grace and love.

Causes can be exceptionally good if they are done in the correct mind and out of the motivation of glorifying the Lord and serving others. But if devotion to God is not the first priority in our actions, then we must realize the obviousness of the truth: if we make "causes" the pursuit of our lives, then we have ceased to truly be devoted to God and instead are devoted to that endeavor above the Lord.

Pursuing things for any other reason than to transform our hearts to the likeness of Christ is a very serious danger to all believers and disciples of Jesus over the entire world because we don't see it as a danger. Or even more dangerous, because we don't notice what we're doing at all. We see doing "good" things, like helping people cross the street or donating money, as an always edifying and holy pursuit. But the truth is that even these "good" things, if done out of the wrong motives and done for any other reason than to become more like Christ, can and will distract us from God.

Does this mean that good deeds are bad and we should not do them or cease our pursuit of holiness? No, not at all. What it does mean is that we should always do our best to keep the Lord our goal and our motivation for all that we do. Because holy actions devoid of our Holy God are nothing but holey actions, empty. Too many times we can all fall into the trap of doing good things for our own personal gain like holding a door for someone so the individuals around you will see how nice of a person you are. Other times we perform good deeds out of habit, without having our heart and mind in the right place at all because such focus and devotion to Christ is difficult to maintain. But good deeds without God are not good, since only God is good—they're just deeds.

Therefore we must always be sure to ask the Lord to examine our hearts so that when we pursue anything, we do so to and for the Lord's glory and not the glory these actions may produce in and of themselves. When Christ sets us free from our sin to live anew He gives us the ability to live again, but this time *for* Him, *of* Him and *through* Him. Because only when we have given everything away and live for Christ do we understand and experience the beauty of real life: genuine, selfless love.

At the mention of giving everything away, I wonder if many of you, if not all of you, immediately thought, "Does he mean my money?" Now, like I said, I do wonder if every one thought this on some level (at least I would have), but rest assured that that is not what I mean unless, of course, your money defines who you are.

Because when I say that you must give everything away to genuinely live for Christ I wasn't talking about what you own, but rather what you are. It's not about giving away what I own when I wish to treasure Christ in my heart and through my actions in life. I give away not what I own, but what I *am* for Jesus. Yet like the young, wealthy ruler who asked Christ what he must do to enter the kingdom of heaven, if your possessions, or anything else for that matter, are what make you who you are and are what you treasure most, than you must give all of them away:

"For what will a man give in exchange for his soul?" –Mark 8:37.

The scariest thing about this kind of divided attention involving good deeds or noble causes is that it can so easily influence the way we view our walk with God. Many of us will eagerly sacrifice our own desires for the "sake" of Christ without realizing that the "causes" for Christ we passionately pursue have replaced Christ at the top of our devotion list.

For instance, having an impeccable church attendance can easily overtake the true reason for attending church: worshipping the Lord. Because the cold, hard fact is that if we give more attention to a pursuit, even a godly pursuit, than to the Lord Jesus Christ—we commit idolatry. When it comes down to it the Lord is not so much concerned with what you are fighting for or how you are fighting, as He is with *whom* you are fighting for, especially if you are not fighting for Him.

What we as a family of God do not need is more individuals who have a godly cause to fight for and an undying devotion to that pursuit. What we must have more of are followers of the Savior who have an undying devotion to God and God alone, even at the expense of their own desires, their own drives and their own causes—even unto death.

In a sense, that is precisely what martyrdom is: to cling so closely to the side of Christ that all you see and distinguish are things either of Christ or things not of Christ. For the Lord Jesus does not so much desire us to plainly die for Him as He desires for us to completely live for Him. And then, if to completely live for Him we must place ourselves in harm's way or even death, we can say that to keep on living for Christ means that we must give up our life and not compromise the complete life we have in Him.

"To live is Christ and to die is gain." –Philippians 1:21.

And unfortunately, as the Bible tells us, sometimes when we stand firm as a people of God and do not compromise our devotion to Christ in this fallen world, we will encounter suffering. But the hope, happiness and joy we have in those harsh times is this: Christ *never* waivers in *His* devotion to us.

A full joy begins with devotion to Christ. And devotion begins by doing three things with your life: *dying daily to the will of others, dying daily to your self-will* and *living daily for the love of Christ.*

DEVOTION MEANS DYING DAILY TO THE WILL OF OTHERS;
HOLDING NO ONE ABOVE OUR LORD JESUS CHRIST.

Immediately after I graduated college I quickly began to pursue a career—any career I could find. As I began to weigh my options, (which, by the way, are very limited for a graduate with an English degree and a minor in History), I slowly lost touch with the Voice of God and began listening to my own ideas of what my purpose was in life. I turned away from my devotion to God and began to use my gifts (that He had given me) for myself. I took on a job as a journalist working for a local newspaper, which *was* exciting and somewhat fulfilling in its own right, but I still felt out of place and out of sync. So I began looking into the possibility of becoming a teacher, which had always been an interest of mine because of some professors that I admired in college.

However, while I was debating and contemplating all the possible paths I could take on an occupational basis, I was subtly ignoring and flat out avoiding the plans and paths that the Lord desired me to walk. I was *trying* to live in God's will without obeying or *seeking* the will of God.

And from that personal experience I learned that sooner or later one of two things happens to you if you turn from seeking His will for your life: first, you become so dissatisfied with your professional endeavors that you are forced to seek the Lord for guidance because you feel so lost. Or the second option, you don't seek the Lord for guidance, despite being dissatisfied with your personal endeavors, and stray even more from His footsteps.

In the second scenario, which is the one that I unfortunately chose, you become so focused upon what would make you happy in your life that you begin to distance yourself from serving God, and your spiritual vision narrows to the point where you do not even see Christ in your life at all. Life becomes an opportunity for you to feel good about yourself and your endeavors and that's all it is at that point. You basically put blinders on, like the ones on a race horse. And instead of running the race set before each of us with purpose and endurance (I'd rather the word be spelled endure-ance as a reminder), you just start dashing and racing endlessly towards a trivial and troublesome goal: self-satisfaction.

And it is at this point, the point of blind ambition towards satisfying the wanton desires of self-fulfillment that God will not allow you to meander off of the path He has chosen for you. But what can He do to get your attention at this point? You're blind. I had become so deaf to His whispers and blind to His moving deep in my heart that God had to resort to the one thing that garners each of our attentions: *pain*. If you remember back in the chapter on prayer, I paraphrased a statement Lewis had made regarding the Lord's last resort to getting through to us. Allow me to share with you C.S. Lewis's deeply true message on pain:

> The human spirit will not even begin to try to surrender self-will as long as all seems to be well with it. Now error and sin both have this property, that the deeper they are the less their victim suspects their existence; they are masked evil. Pain is unmasked, unmistakable evil; every man knows that something is wrong when he is being hurt. ...
>
> And pain is not only immediately recognizable evil, but evil impossible to ignore. We can rest contentedly in our sins and in our stupidities; and anyone who has watched gluttons shoveling down the most exquisite foods

as if they did not know they were eating, will admit that we can ignore even pleasure.

But pain insists upon being attended to. God whispers to us in our pleasures, speaks in our conscience, but shouts in our pain: it is His megaphone to rouse a deaf world. [33]

And when your eyes become so accustomed to living in utter darkness, which is what life is for the child of God who has turned astray, even the slightest sliver of light is excruciating. So in my blindness to God and my own foolish quest for control of my life and my pleasure/success, I now feel that is when Jesus grabbed the megaphone:

"I don't want to do this, my child, my friend, but you leave me no choice: *misery!*"

I began to suffer from horrible bouts of misery and depression. Here's the worst part: I still didn't listen. I dismissed my anguish and desolation as bi-products of not getting enough rest or not exercising anymore. So I began sleeping longer and exercised more.

"*MISERY*" resonated even louder in my life.

It is only now in retrospect that I fully appreciate my wife and my family for choosing to be around me and loving me during those dark days of my irritable spirit and anguished soul. Despite the misery, however self-induced it may have been, I always felt the slight echo of Christ calling out to my very-being, "Please my brother, my friend, seek me and I will make you whole."

The megaphone of God finally sank in for me at a church service on a Sunday in October. The pastor's message was about purpose and how there can be no joy or happiness without the hand of Christ moving you and sustaining you. And that's when I finally regained my sight.

"Oh, I'm so dense," I said. "How could I not have seen this before? How could I have been so—blind?"

So as I *finally* realized what my grand error had been, I began to experience a tremendous amount of relief and joy, but joy mixed with a tinge of sorrow. Because what I had not realized throughout the entire affair, was that not only had *I* been hurting and in anguish, but that I had been hurting the Lord. As any parent knows, when your child runs out into the street without your permission, you are forced to punish and discipline them because of it. Any sadness they go through or tears they cry is twice as painful upon your heart because you hate to make your child unhappy even if it is for their own good.

And that is precisely what I had done to the Lord. I had made Him put pain in my life in order to protect me from an even greater pain: distancing myself from His loving side.

No matter where you are in your walk with God or what you are doing in your life, if you are not completely devoted to Jesus above all else then you are *not* devoted to Christ:

"So because you are lukewarm, and neither hot nor cold, I will spit you out of My mouth." –Revelation 3:16.

And the horrible reality is that you are not only hurting yourself by creating a division between you and the Lord, but you hurt Him as well.

> DEVOTION MEANS DYING DAILY TO OUR SELF-WILL;
> TO NOT USE OUR "TALENTS" FOR OURSELVES.

To surrender to the grace of God *is* to lay everything at His feet. Every professing Christian to ever walk this earth must know this truth deep down in their hearts, according to the Word of God. But the concept of devotion and the application of it onto our daily lives is much more difficult to grasp.

This does not mean just laying our troubles and tribulations at the feet of Christ in order to surrender to His grace. We must give up our strengths and successes to Him as well. As we can all probably agree, it's usually quite a natural response to dump our struggles and weaknesses onto the cross of Jesus Christ when we're in times of trouble. But to surrender it all means to give up our *strengths and abilities* to Him as well, which is a much more difficult thing to do.

Within the parable of the talents, found in Matthew 25: 14-30, we find just how difficult a death it is for an individual to surrender to their master their talents in devoted service and obedience:

"For it [the coming of the Lord] is just like a man about to go on a journey, who called his own slaves and entrusted his possessions to them. To one he gave five talents, to another, two, and another, one, each according to his own ability; and he went on his journey.

Immediately the one who had received the five talents went and traded with them, and gained five more talents. In the same manner the one who had received the two talents gained two more.

But he who received the one talent went away, and dug a hole in the ground and hid his master's money."

What happens when you stick something into the ground?

Well if you have a dog, the dog will dig up whatever it is you stuck in the ground and you will have to place it back in the ground. Thus the process repeats itself over and over again and so it would be better, usually, to not bury things in the ground in the first place if you own a dog; without a dog they'll just stay there. So what's with all the dog references?

Here's why. I'd like to use an illustration that describes the Holy Spirit of God as having doglike qualities, but before you ridicule me, laugh or gasp in shock, allow me to further explain the metaphor. In our lives we have the tendency and desire to not utilize our gifts for the glory of the Lord, but to use them only for ourselves, or some other cause. And so, much like the third slave who was only given one talent, instead of using our God-given gifts for the Person who bestowed them upon us, we stick them in the ground so that only we can use them.

And it is here that the Spirit of God is like a dog: no matter how often you dig a hole in the ground and bury the talent that God has given you into that dark, hidden hole, the Holy Spirit will always dig it right back up and place it into your conscience with a note saying, "Return to Sender."

No matter how many times you try to use your talents for yourself, Christ will always beckon you to use them for His glory; it is only when we use them for the glory of Christ, which results in using them for the people around us, that we experience the fullness of that God-given talent. The Holy Spirit consistently draws to your attention the gifts He has given you that you are not using for Him.

So, back to that third slave. Can you imagine being handed a diamond encrusted item of jewelry, and then going and sticking it in the ground to protect it from being damaged?

Doesn't that sound ridiculous? Trying to use a gift that the Lord has given you for your own personal gain is exactly what the third slave did when he buried the talent into the ground. Because it is only when we use our talents in devotion to Christ and in His name that our talents ever truly shine, because for anything to ever genuinely shine in this life it must radiate with the majesty and Light of God.

Woe to the man or woman who doesn't do everything they can with the talent the Maker has graciously laid into the palm of their hands! Can you imagine a greater insult than to refuse to make the most of what God has given you? But that is *precisely* what the third slave did and what many of us do, in fact what I was doing, in search of self-fulfillment. "But he who received the one talent went away, and dug a hole in the ground and hid his master's money."

So what happened to the third slave after the first and second slaves handed their master double what he gave them:

"Now after a long time the master of those slaves came and settled accounts with them[…]And the one also who had received the one talent came up and said, 'Master, I knew you to be a hard man, reaping where you did not sow and gather where you scattered no seed. And I was afraid, and went away and hid your talent in the ground. See, you have what is yours.'

But his master answered and said to him, 'You wicked, lazy slave, you knew that I reap where I did not sow and gather where I scattered no seed. Then you ought to have put my money in the bank, and on my arrival I would have received my money back with interest. Therefore take away the talent from him, and give it to the one who has the ten talents.

'For to everyone who has, more shall be given, and he will have an abundance; but from the one who does not have, even what he does have shall be taken away.

'Throw out the worthless slave into the outer darkness; in that place there will be weeping and gnashing of teeth." –Matthew 25:14-30.

When I withheld my "talent" or my skills from the Lord in an effort to provide myself with happiness, the Lord really did take everything away from me until I realized my sin.

So in what ways can we surrender our desire for success and fulfillment in life unto Christ? How can we have true devotion by dying every day to our self-will? Well, there are two concrete ways that you can surrender your self-will on a daily basis: invest your talents into others so that they might better glorify God and use whatever skills you have to your utmost and *do so* for the glory of God.

The master describes the first way when he tells his slave, "You wicked, lazy slave, you knew that I reap where I did not sow and gather where I scattered no seed. Then you ought to have put my money in the bank, and on my arrival I would have received my money back with interest."

The Lord Jesus gives each of us specific abilities and gifts so that we may do the most wonderful and bewildering thing of all: the work of God. Why God entrusts us with His service and His purpose can sometimes make any believer sincerely question the decision-making skills of a perfect God who lays His work into the hands of imperfect people. But that is what God has chosen to do, chosen to bless us with every day.

So why does God do it? One of the reasons is so we will depend upon each other and seek fellowship with one another because only through the investing of our own uniquely separate gifts can we ever grow (discussed further in later chapters). Also, let us use parents for our next example. When an individual achieves success it is a great blessing and feeling. But when a parent sees their child achieve success and glory, there's not a blessing or feeling to top it. The same goes when a teacher watches his student accomplish the "impossible." That is how I believe God feels when we use what He has given us to achieve the greatest accomplishment ever: glorifying Him. That, I believe, is why He has given us *all* little gifts of Himself.

And it is in this revelation that the word of the master in the parable makes sense. You see, the Lord does not physically reap the benefits of the seeds we sow with our gifts (He gives us the opportunity to do that), but in the end, as the parable shows us, everything belongs to the Lord. And as it is our responsibility to utilize what He has given us, it is also our responsibility to invest our gifts into the lives of others.

This is one of the possible things I think was meant by "put my money in the bank, and on my arrival I would have received my money back with interest." Whenever you invest your time and skills into the life of someone else, the blessings that result in that are two times the amount they would have been had you only used your own skills for God's glory. Because by investing in the lives and growth of someone else, you not only bless Jesus, but you bless that person as well, who then goes on glorifying Christ.

Devotion to Christ really is a complete death to our desire to control our own life:

"Hence the necessity to die daily: however often we think we have broken the rebellious self we shall still find [that rebellious self] alive." –C.S. Lewis. [34]

When we begin dying daily to self, we begin giving our life away to others out of love for them and for the Lord's glory, which is exactly what Christ did for us. He poured out all of His desires and talents to the Father for our sanctification and glory: "…so that My joy may be in you, and that your joy may be made full." –John 16:24.

In essence, Christ sacrificed His everything so that we may in return pour out everything of ourselves to Him and others for His glory!

DEVOTION IS LIVING DAILY IN CHRIST. HALLELUJAH!

One of my favorite verses in the Bible is Galatians 2:20:

"I have been crucified with Christ; and it is no longer I who live but Christ lives in me; and the life which I now live in the flesh I live by faith in the Son of God, who loved me and gave Himself up for me."

There are some individuals who believe that Christ actually desired to be crucified or sacrificed and in turn ask me, "Did He really give Himself up for me then?" I have always advised those individuals, with gentleness in my finer moments and not arguments or complete shock, which are present in my not-so-fine moments, to carefully reread Scripture. And the verse I always point them to is of course Luke 22:42, when Christ asked the Lord in Gethsemane:

"Father, if You are willing, remove this cup from Me; yet not My will, but Yours be done."

Christ did not *want* to pursue the cause of the cross, but He did so nonetheless. Now the Lord Jesus was definitely strong to choose that path, yet the strength He had to make such a miraculous decision was based on His unfathomable devotion and dependence upon the grace of the Father. Christ trusted in the will of God for His life and the love that His Father had for Him. The Son of God sacrificed His abilities and desires to and for the will of the Father—to and for our redemption. Christ pursued the will (the cause) of God above everything, even His very life.

And in the process, He brought salvation and hope to all of mankind.

So then, the real question about how to live daily in Christ is not about what gifts God *can* give or *has* given to you so that you can live a successful and luxurious life, but asking the Lord Jesus, "What do You desire me to do, Lord, with the life and gifts you've given me?" Devotion is not about asking for the "right" gifts from God, but using whatever gifts you have for Jesus.

Stop for a moment and ask yourself when was the only time that you didn't focus on wanting more out of your life. Those rare moments in my own life have only been found when I wasn't focusing on my life at all but when nothing could rip my eyes or loving stare off of the person of Jesus Christ. The only times I have ever felt fulfilled was when I was filled with His Holy Spirit and the wonder and awe of such presence. When your eyes are overcome with the glory of His love and majesty shining down upon you, you no longer are searching for a successfully luxurious life because true life is surrounding you. When you look for anything other than Him, you'll find everything but Him.

After suffering through that time of depression and seeking self-fulfillment, I did finally ask the Lord what He wanted me to do with the gifts He had given me. And through that devotion and dependence to His hands for guidance, I found fulfillment. A fulfillment found only by the Lord correcting my false assumptions regarding devotion. Before I sought Him earnestly for purpose and direction, I thought that the answer to a lukewarm life was vivacious and energetic living. But what I came to realize is the eternal truth that resides within total devotion to the Lord Jesus: The cure to a mediocre walk with God is not intensity, no matter how deep or extravagant, but truth, no matter how small or common.

Because a true life of devotion is not about excitement or greatness, but pure focus *on* and love *of* Jesus—no matter what that life may look like. One of the best examples of this is the quite hidden life and work of Brother Andrew.

"In 1955 a young Dutch missionary named Brother Andrew went on a group tour to Poland. There he discovered a remnant of a church behind the Iron Curtain desperately in need of the Word of God. Brother Andrew distributed a suitcase full of Christian literature behind the Iron Curtain." Fifty years later, Brother Andrew has arguably been one of the most influential Christian missionaries ever—despite being relatively *unknown*.

"Brother Andrew's one-man operation quickly broadened to delivering Bibles in China, Vietnam and later Africa and the Muslim World, along with organizing training seminars and supplying practical aid for suffering Christians. He and his affiliate organization, Open Doors, are working in more than 45 countries to strengthen the Persecuted Church, and sustaining indigenous Christians in hostile lands so they can continue to spread the Gospel to the unsaved majority around them. His underground network of indigenous Christians has aided in the secret distribution of millions of Bibles each year worldwide. Open Doors has trained thousands of Christian pastors and church leaders, assisted in economic relief, literacy training, and vocational training in the most dangerous countries in the world from China to the war-torn Sudan and even to the volatile Middle East." [35]

But to the majority of the population *including* Christians, we have never heard of Brother Andrew and would not recognize him if he was sitting right next to us. It is not Brother Andrew's work in hiddenness or relative obscurity that affect so many, but the true life of devotion within him, the complete surrender and commitment to Jesus Christ above everything, that impacts millions of people to follow Christ. Millions of people who will probably never know that Brother Andrew's obedient focus *on* and love *of* the Lord is the reason they can read their Bibles.

That kind of devotion will forever fulfill us and aid others because that kind of devotion overflows with the love and power of Jesus Christ.

Application:

For the next week, try to see every event, every moment in obedience to Jesus. Concentrate on how He would desire you to act and to speak.

This is, in essence, what the very popular "W.W.J.D.? (What Would Jesus Do?)" arm bracelets were asking each of us every time we glanced their way or put them onto our wrists. Now these may have become mere jewelry to many or a fashionable accessory, but their inner, true message still rings true. In fact, the question of "What would Christ will for me to do?" rings deep into each of us as to how we are going to live the next moment of our lives.

If you catch yourself focusing upon what you want or what you will get out of a situation, turn your eyes back to Christ and just focus upon the words of Jesus, "not My will but Yours be done." And remember that if anything, even if it is a good and noble cause, becomes more of your focus and motivation than to serve and glorify God, you, we, all of us, need to refocus our priorities.

Being totally and passionately devoted to Jesus Christ is the greatest gift you can offer the Lord and even more so, the greatest gift you can offer yourself. Because to live in Christ is to die to the darkness of discouraging pain, since He alone is our joy and hope.

Prayer:

Most gracious and loving Father God, I thank You for the devotion and love You show us every single day of our lives. That despite our sin and rebellion from Your sovereign guidance, Lord, You never leave us nor forsake us. I humbly ask that You would give us the strength, Your strength of Spirit, to help us keep our eyes completely on You when we walk out our door every day. I ask that our devotion be not divided, but entirely fixed upon Your will and face, Lord Jesus. Let us not be lukewarm for You, but instead grant us the grace to be a consuming fire in Your will, Father God, so that all of those who see us, see Your face and Your grace. Our hope, Lord, is that through our unrelenting devotion to You, Jesus, others may come to place their devoted heart fully into Your hands. I ask all these things in the precious and powerful name of Jesus, and for Your sake always, Lord. Amen!

Chapter Nine

The Forgetting of Self: Service

> *"Let a man regard us in this manner, as servants of Christ and stewards of the mysteries of God."*
> —The Apostle Paul

> *"As each one has received a spiritual gift, employ it in serving one another as good stewards of the manifold grace of God. Whoever speaks, is to do so as one who is speaking the utterances of God; whoever serves is to do so as one who is serving by the strength which God supplies; so that in all things God may be glorified through Jesus Christ, whom belongs the glory and dominion forever and ever. Amen."*
> —Simon Peter

Their feet were covered in dust, caked with manure, and calloused from years of labor and walking. The stench alone was enough to make your eyes water and your nostrils burn when they raised their feet up onto the table that you were about to eat off of in a few moments. But somebody had to clean the feet before dinner. Someone had to be the person who degraded and lowered himself by touching these cracked and disgusting feet. Someone had to be the one to place his hands into a bowl of water mixed with mule dung, dirt and desert sand. Somebody had to be the one to either swallow their pride and do it—or make someone else do it instead.

The washing of feet was one of the most menial chores that existed. The only people who were forced or called upon to clean and wash the feet of individuals were slaves or citizens of the lower class. It can be argued that never before in the history of mankind had anyone who had his feet washed ever felt unworthy while the task was being performed.

Until Christ did it for the apostles.

And no matter how stained and repulsive their feet may have been that night, the last night that Christ would spend with His disciples, His friends, the disciple's feet were no match for the state of our soul before a Heavenly and Pristine God. So what did the Perfect and Spotless Son of God do when confronted with such disgusting wretchedness, both spiritual and physical?

He lowered to His knees and washed them, us, one by one. He lowered His holy hands into the water and washed their revolting feet, stained Himself, so that He could pull us out on the other side *clean*.

I've always wished that I could have seen the eyes of the apostles as Jesus washed their feet. Can you imagine it? How would you react? How would you feel as the Lord of all creation stooped to one knee, grabbed your disgusting foot and looked at you with *love* in His eyes?

When Christ humbled Himself during the washing of feet the apostles all caught a glimpse of a true and loving servant, a true and loving God. Because the King of kings showed each of them, each of us, just what a real king is. A genuine king does not concern himself with how he might best be served by his subjects, but only with how he can best serve the citizens in his kingdom. It is uniquely within Christ that we see an authentic, heavenly King vividly serve. Only Jesus volunteered for sacrifice when all of heaven stood silent. It is only Christ who stepped out of heaven and placed Himself into the dark, dark water of this world, this flesh and our sin.

"God is the Infinite Servant. God is the most humble being in all the universe. Jesus did not come as a servant *in spite of* the fact that he is God; he came *precisely because of* the fact that he is God" –John Ortberg [36]

He did it because He loved us, to make us clean when we did not deserve washing. And it is that self-sacrifice, that willingness to do what no one else will for the sake of others, that makes Christ the King!

There is probably not a more powerful event or closing verse in the entire realm of Scripture than the last line of the event of the washing of the disciple's feet in John 13: 8:

"Peter said to Him, 'Never shall You wash my feet!' Jesus answered Him, 'If I do not wash you, you have no part with Me."

Allow me to paraphrase what I believe that the Lord was saying to Peter:

If I do not wash you, [If I do not give up My life and suffer, If I do not bleed on the cross of Calvary] you have no part with Me [because only I can cleanse you, only I am willing to serve no matter what the cost—to see you again in heaven]."

Christ showed the apostles and all of creation the greatest love there is for another: *selfless service*. If humility is genuinely glorifying the Lord and devotion is having true loyalty to the Lord, then servanthood means truly loving the Lord. Having the hands, and more importantly, the heart of a servant, is to have humility and devotion beautifully joined together in love for Christ. Because when you are humble enough to give Christ all the glory and devoted enough to let nothing compromise your place at His side, then the next action you will naturally take is to show Christ your love, which is what we today call *service*.

The Three Ways Service Edifies the Kingdom of God

As Christ showed us through the washing of the disciples' feet, there are three essential purposes found in serving the Lord and others that enable us to live a life drenched in the Holy Spirit: *service helps us focus solely on Jesus, helps others see Christ by being an example* and *helps us become more like Christ by giving Him all the glory.*

SERVING HELPS US FOCUS SOLELY ON JESUS AND NOTHING ELSE

Before Christ washed the disciples' feet, the fickle concerns and priorities of man reared their ugly head. In this moment, after the *last meal* with their Lord and Savior, the disciples got into a debate over which one of them was the greatest. The dispute between the disciples immediately following the Lord's Supper is perhaps the most powerful depiction of humanity's unbelievable obsession with our own importance. Sounds a bit too familiar does it not? Painfully familiar, unfortunately.

Far too often in my life have I been too busy making sure I look like the greatest disciple instead of preparing myself, this fleshly "upper room," for the presence of the Lamb of God. The fact that many of us have been missing all along is that honor does not exist without the grace of God. And genuine, Christ-like honor can't be found in appearances or even in leadership roles, but in the man or woman who willingly sacrifices their dignity to do the task that no one else will even contemplate doing. Greatness abides only in serving God and His children.

"The one who is greatest among you must become like the youngest, and the leader like the servant. For who is greater, the one who reclines at the table or the one who serves? Is it not the one who reclines at the table? But I am among you as the one who serves." –Luke 22:26

In this verse Jesus gives us a real good look at what an authentic leader looks like because, despite Christ being beyond a shadow of a doubt "the greater one" in our relationship with Him, He does not "recline at the table." Not at all. Christ is "among you [us] as the one who serves."

So we can now see that the one who has authority and prestige in a situation should not be "reclining at the table" waiting to be served by those who are "less" than they are, but rather should be serving the individuals around them so that they might not only recognize what godly leadership looks like, but serve the individuals in their lives.

Then why don't we?

Well, one answer is that we all like to feel powerful and superior to other people. This is an unfortunate truth that we all must crucify daily if we ever have real aspirations and commitments to becoming a servant of God. Feelings of spiritual superiority or authority, that so many people cling to, are our twisted form of God's beautiful gift of serving. Much like the way quicksand is a twisted form of a beach; instead of leading you into refreshing waters it subtly swallows you whole.

So why then is humble service the way of heaven? Well a simple answer is that this is how the Lord Jesus Christ was and is. He came to serve, not be served. Despite being the Sovereign King of mankind, the Messiah did not come to have mankind cater to Him. Instead He got down on His knees *because* He was and is the King of mankind. Remember that that is what a true king or leader does. They don't look to be served; they look for ways *to* serve.

A more in-depth glance into the responsibility of a man or woman of God begins to show us what Jesus already knew: the conceited importance we place upon ourselves will always strangle the Holy Spirit's ability to love and edify us. Why? Because we won't follow or obey when the Holy Spirit leads us. Because the only appetite self-glorification and self-serving (vanity, vanity, vanity) feed is an unending starvation.

Vanity truly is a famine that tries to fill itself with the sinful sustenance of pride. Ironically, though, the entire time we are trying to find fulfillment through acclaim or feelings of power or authority over others, we quietly starve, yearning for the only "food" that satisfies the soul: the bread of Christ. All too often, however, we end up settling for the poison of temporary esteem and false supremacy.

In stark contrast, the mindset of a servant is the only path that leads towards actions of the true humility we've talked about. Because only within those selfless deeds of service do we really fix our focus solely on glorifying God through the work of serving everyone, but ourselves.

"Then Jesus said to His disciples, 'If anyone wishes to come after Me, he must deny himself, and take up his cross and follow Me. For whoever wishes to save his life will lose it; but whoever loses his life for My sake will find it." –Matthew 16:24-25.

To become like Christ is to forever place the limelight on others so that you may shine in the meek and quiet splendor of glorifying the Lord. So to answer the question of the arguing apostles: Who is the greatest? Christ Jesus is! And His selfless service for our souls shook the foundations of the earth, conquered death and sin, and showed each of us just how much love was given on that cross.

Why not follow the greatest?

SERVING HELPS US BE AN EXAMPLE TO OTHERS OF THE LOVE AND SELFLESSNESS OF CHRIST.

"Do you know what I have done to you? You call me Teacher and Lord; and you are right, for so I am. If I, then, the Lord and the Teacher, washed your feet, you also ought to wash one another's feet. For I gave you an example that you also should do as I did to you." –John 13: 12b-15

The majority of people who walk this planet have an incorrect idea about what love really is; especially Christians! The reason I say especially is because despite having the very example of love, our Lord, we still believe love is either a feeling, or a desire, or a distant, theological concept. But by no means do any of those things accurately represent the face of love, Jesus Christ! Love does not depend upon how much you feel in your heart, but how you live your life.

And here is where the servant reveals the true nature of love by showing, through his or her selfless deeds, the nature of Christ's gracious heart. Because the liberty we have been given by the sacrifice of Christ does not mean we have license to do whatever we feel in our heart, or desire, or think, but rather we have been given freedom to serve God and one another through His love:

"For you were called to freedom, brethren, only do not turn your freedom into an opportunity for the flesh but through love serve one another. For the whole Law is fulfilled in one word, in the statement, 'You shall love your neighbor as yourself.'" –Galatians 5:13-14.

Only when you give up serving yourself and begin to serve only Jesus out of love for Him, do you find limitless, everlasting freedom. To gain freedom we must all give up our desire to be free. Christ embodied this truth completely as He lowered to one knee in both an act of instruction, and divine love. Being an example of Christ through service will allow us to help guide others into a closer faith with Jesus by *building each other up, by serving one another with our individual talents* and *by being examples of physical and spiritual service.*

First, serving helps us edify the family of God. We are all given different gifts so that we might serve each other and in doing so, provide each other with skills and insights that we could never receive on our own, as Ephesians 4:7-13 tells us:

But to each one of us grace was given according to the measure of Christ's gift [...] And He gave some as apostles, and some as prophets, and some as evangelists, and some as pastors and teachers, for the equipping of the saints for the work of service, to the building up of the body of Christ; until we all attain to the unity of the faith, and of the knowledge of the Son of God, to a mature man, to the measure of the stature which belongs to the fullness of Christ.

The reason God made you exactly the way you are is not so you can use your God-given talents (here comes devotion's influence on service) individualistically. No, you were given those talents to use them to their fullest, and that is only possible by serving God, which includes building up the body of believers so that we can all grow together into the likeness of Christ! So that we can experience Spirit-breathed unity and fullness of the family of God (and that is how service influences our next chapter: Fellowship).

Secondly, one of the amazing things about serving is that there are as many ways of displaying Christ to those around us as there are Christians. For instance, look at Romans 12:1:

"Therefore I urge you, brethren, by the mercies of God, to present your bodies a living and holy sacrifice, acceptable to God, which is your *spiritual service* of worship" (emphasis added)

What this tells us is that servanthood does not just entail physical acts of performing deeds or tasks, but the spiritual as well.

To be holy and righteous in the sight of God is *an act of service*. And to be holy and righteous in the sight of God and in the sight of men will also show other children of God how to pursue the "spiritual service of worship."

Serving enables us to become more like Christ by giving Him all the glory

"More than any other single way the grace of humility is worked into our lives through the Discipline of service...Nothing disciplines the inordinate desires of the flesh like service, and nothing transforms the desires of the flesh like serving in hiddenness. The flesh whines against service but screams against hidden service. It strains and pulls for honor and recognition." – Richard Foster [37]

When we "discipline the desires of the flesh" through service we are also allowing the desires of the Spirit to move and mold us into the image of Christ. And since Christ was the penultimate servant, it is obvious that to become more like Christ, which is the entire goal of Christianity, we should probably take a gander at this whole servant thing.

Now I say that jokingly, but I can not stress the seriousness of this Scriptural truth. If you have any desire in your heart to grow in your relationship with Christ and become more like Him and less like yourself then you must develop and maintain the heart of a servant throughout your life. To keep Jesus as Lord of our lives we all must not only obey His commandments but try not to take back control of our lives from Him (or else He really wouldn't be Lord and Ruler of our lives).

And the *only* way to make sure you keep Christ as Lord of your life is to become His servant every day. When people are so enamored and concentrated on doing the will of their Lord, they don't have time to take control of their life. Sadly though, many children of God are trying to hand Christ the keys of their life and invite Him into the driver's seat while wrestling with Him for control of the wheel from the back seat.

What they, and we, don't realize is that when we are wrestling with Christ for control of our lives we never truly allow Him to guide us. In effect, it's like Christ is driving us down the road of discipleship dodging the setbacks and potholes along the way. But instead of continually strapping ourselves in the backseat of the car we begin struggling with Him for the right to drive. And so what happens? When the potholes come, we are so busy fighting for control that we don't allow the Lord to guide us past them. So we skid off the side of the road and into a giant mud puddle; we get stuck in the mire of trying to be lord of our lives...again.

If we are to serve Jesus we must follow His example and the path of His life: one of continual servitude no matter how degrading or trivial. Following Christ, as He told us, means that we must pro-actively seek opportunities to serve others around us and not just "recline at the table" for the activities we enjoy to fall at our feet. As any coach will tell you, the players who make the biggest impact on not only the game, but in their community and in other players' lives, is normally the athlete with the biggest heart and not the one with the greatest talent. In a sense, we are all players and teammates on the Lord's team and just like athletes on the field, the most impact that any of us will make for Christ through service will be because of our heart, for Him and each other. Real service is born out of a desire to help, not out of a desire to do what you want. If you only did what you wanted to do and never for the aid of others, could you really call that service? Did Christ only do what He wanted to do? Definitely not!

The role of a servant can be easily seen through the metaphor of kitchen utensils. Every utensil in your kitchen has a specific purpose and is thus designed to efficiently perform a specific job. From a spatula to a cheese grater, these utensils make it easier for you to cook than if you only had one tool to use for every dish. Now for myself, I only use one pot and a spatula to make eggs and macaroni and cheese (which is the full extent of my culinary repertoire), however there are a plethora of other devices that make cooking not only easier, but also a joy. Yet, utensils that are not in the kitchen can't be used now can they?

The servant of God who is not pro-actively and deliberately looking for ways to be used by God through the service of others will not be selected by the Lord. It's that simple. No matter how sharp a knife may be, no matter how perfectly constructed the blade is, if the knife is not able or around to do the job then you (and especially the Lord) can't, and more importantly, *won't*, use it to feed the hungry children of God. Christ will use whatever tool is at His disposal and ready to be used, which is sometimes the one that is not best suited to the job but is willing to do anything that is asked. Just like an absent knife, Christ will use a wooden spoon to cut and feed others (service) as long as, no, *especially* because the spoon is willing.

A willing tool, a willing servant is the greatest instrument to a loving God because the servant is ready and *eager* to do whatever is asked of him or her, instead of just waiting to use what talents they may possess when the moment arises. An eagerness to serve will always prevail over the ability to serve because many individuals are able to serve and don't, yet it is uniquely within the man and woman who are eager to serve no matter what may be asked of them, that the Holy Spirit empowers them and changes lives; the lives of not only the eager servants but more so, the lives of the individuals they serve.

The reason that the eager servants' lives are changed is because through their readiness to do the will of God, no matter what that might entail, they begin to more accurately reflect and thus authentically become more transformed into the image of Christ. This genuine reflection of Jesus is seldom seen but even more seldom forgotten when witnessed. The reason the lives of the individuals they serve are changed is because they witness this powerful "little Christ," which is what the word "Christian" actually means. The person of Jesus Christ and the presence of the Holy Spirit are indeed life-altering, even when it is within us that others see Christ and through our service hear the gentle whispers of the Holy Spirit.

Jesus became the greatest servant to walk this earth when He sacrificed His will and died upon the cross—serving God. That is precisely what Christ calls each of us to do: take up our cross daily and crucify our lives by serving Him and each other.

"He who loves his life loses it, and he who hates his life in this world will keep it to life eternal. If anyone serves Me, he must follow Me; and where I am, there My servant will be also; if anyone serve Me, the Father will honor him" –John 12:25-26.

Application:
SERVE.

Humble yourself to do the menial tasks and chores and to go out of your way for someone else. Through service we are brought a heartbeat's distance from the pulse of Jesus. Do not be concerned with, in fact fight and actively resist, how others view your service or what you can receive out of it. If you focus on that then you might as well not have served at all. But do not let even that fear of giving in to self-glory deter you from service, but use it as fuel to keep you centered on serving the Lord. Surrender that fear to God and thus serve Him by serving everyone but yourself.

Also, remember to pro-actively seek opportunities to serve others around you and not just "recline at the table" for the activities you enjoy doing to fall at your feet. Real service is born out of a desire to help, not out of a desire to do what we want. If you know someone needs your help but you don't really want to do it, then that is the perfect opportunity to genuinely serve the Lord by helping your neighbor.

Prayer:

Most gracious and loving Father God we thank You for serving us despite the consequences and suffering that service to us entailed. We can never offer up enough praise to adequately thank You for the gift of eternal life Your service granted us, but let us, Lord, offer our thanks to You through the act of serving others. Please help us to stay focused on others and You and not ourselves. This is a very difficult task, Jesus, and can only be accomplished through Your Holy Spirit moving in our hearts and keeping us centered upon Your righteousness and leadership. I thank You that You gave us the perfect example of how to serve with the very image of Your life and even Your death. Let us follow the greatest Father God! Guide us so that we follow the Lord Jesus Christ! In His precious name and for His sake always, Amen.

PART FOUR

*Living a Life of Love:
Becoming a Reflection of
the Lord Jesus Christ*

Chapter Ten
The Family of God: Fellowship

> *"Abide in Me, and I in you. As the branch cannot bear fruit of itself unless it abides in the vine, so neither can you unless you abide in Me. I am the vine, you are the branches, he who abides in Me and I in him, he bears much fruit, for apart from Me you can do nothing [...] Just as the Father has loved Me, I have loved you; abide in my love."*
> —Jesus of Nazareth

> *"If we say that we have fellowship with Him and yet walk in the darkness, we lie and do not practice the truth; but if we walk in the Light as He Himself is in the Light, we have fellowship with one another, and the blood of Jesus His Son cleanses us from all sin."*
> —John the Beloved

Diana's church group is having a get together at her house around 7:00 p.m. So she cleans up her small house the best she can. She puts the chips and dip on the counter and buries soda (also known as pop) cans deep into the ice in the cooler. As the first member of her church group rings the doorbell Diana puts on the smile of a hostess as she welcomes everyone in.

The customary "Hello" is exchanged and various comments on how cold it is outside dominate the various other hellos she and her guests share with each other. As everyone sits down in the living room there is laughter and talk of career and family, but many individuals can only eye the kitchen because they are quite hungry (then again, who really wouldn't?).

Diana invites everyone in after some of the people had already begun making their way into the kitchen and have steadily hovered around the food (I myself have been a hoverer more times than I can remember). After dinner, they play a few games and discuss the church and how the minister really should have cleared his throat at the beginning of the message Sunday instead of struggling through it like a frog with strep.

Eventually individuals have had enough camaraderie and begin to miss the quiet solitude of their own living room and so give the customary "Thanks for having us" as they shuffle out the front door. As Diana walks with the last guest to the front door, the young woman about to leave does not give Diana any of the usual closing goodbyes. Instead, she makes a simple statement.

"This was a great fellowship we had, Diana."

And as Diana prepares to respond, a thought suddenly hangs over her like a thick fog in the winter. *Fellowship.* Diana tries to smile or respond as the young woman walks out the door, but can't. The long groan of the large oak door and the quick click of the bronze lock mimics the epiphany taking place in Diana's heart.

Fellowship…

When tonight did we experience fellowship?

What does fellowship mean to you?

The odds are that fellowship is more of a definition of a term to you than a specific experience you hold dear to your heart. In fact, it is most likely that fellowship really doesn't have an exact meaning in your life because you have heard the word used and defined as so many different things. But fellowship does mean something very important and very real for believers in Christ. Especially to God.

The popular thought throughout modern Christianity today is that fellowship is just another synonym for a relationship, but it's definitely not. Fellowship is not just a relationship. It's more than a relationship. It's not just relating to another person. Fellowship is a real relationship.

A real relationship between two followers of Christ, which is what fellowship ultimately fosters, is an ever-growing and edifying interaction between one person and another; between one person and their God. This is why I fear that fellowship may have lost its potency in our lives and Christian gatherings because we don't necessarily see fellowship as cultivating vibrant, living relationships. In some regards life truly is all about relationships (most importantly having one with the Lord), but a relationship is not a stagnant, unchanging thing like a mountain (they don't move and are cold, stone). A relationship is like a swift stream, ever-moving, ever-changing and hopefully—ever-growing in depth.

We see fellowship as something we do or something that happens of its own accord whenever we get together but that is not what the Word of God tells us fellowship is. Fellowship does not happen just when believers gather, *but only when* they gather in the presence of God's Holy Spirit:

"For where two or three have gathered together *in My name*, I am there in their midst." –Matthew 18:20 (emphasis added)

Only when we gather in the name of Christ do we experience true fellowship with each other because that is the only time when we as believers have fellowship with the Spirit of God together. But gathering in the name of Christ is more than saying a prayer before you eat or coming together as a collection of Christians. To gather in the name of Christ is to be there with the intent of opening up your heart for His presence to be in your "midst," for Christ to inhabit your conversations, for Jesus to *be* your gathering.

And when Christ comes into our midst, when the Holy Spirit of God fills more than a room but the hearts of His children, His family, no one who is there could ever mistake the true nature and power of fellowship with the Almighty for a mere meeting of acquaintances. Authentic fellowship is becoming one with the Holy Spirit and thus becoming a part of the family of God. And we are a family of God as Oswald Chambers reveals in *My Utmost for His Highest*:

"When love or the Spirit of God come upon a person, he is transformed. He will then no longer insist on maintaining his individuality…once your rights to yourself are surrendered to God, your true personal nature begins responding to God immediately.

Jesus Christ brings freedom to your total person, and even your individuality is transformed. The transformation is brought about by love—personal devotion to Jesus. Love is the overflowing result of one person in true fellowship with another." –December 12th [38]

The true depth behind what two individuals experience through a Spirit-fed fellowship with one another dwarfs what any of us would ever call a simple "friendship." The word fellowship as you can see takes its root from the word fellow, which is a loving term that a person calls someone they feel understands them and shares their same drives, affections and purpose. And the coming together of fellow believers also produces a unique affection towards the Lord. And since fellowship in the Spirit often happens when two people are not just acquaintances or even close friends, but like minds, we can see that fellowship inspires and sustains the bond that two people share when they are, above all else, companions of the Living God.

An important aspect of genuine fellowship resides in the bond between two believers that is not necessarily typical of all believers. For instance, Peter and Paul were both apostles but each one had a very different connection to the Lord Jesus and to other believers as well. Companionship must have an attachment between the two children of God that surpasses conversations about sports, or television shows or the customary "How are you doing?—I'm fine.—What about you?—I'm good."

A companion is someone who knows you in a way that exceeds mere head knowledge or information about you. The Lord Jesus Christ had this effect on the people around Him as He was and is our *ultimate* companion. A companion is an accountability partner born not out of guilt, but complete honesty and respect. He or she is a person who inspires you and aides you in becoming more like Jesus. A companion sticks with you during the rough spots because they place more confidence in knowing your heart than trying to understand or judge your actions.

A companion will never leave you or forsake you, because in this Christian life, as you're probably beginning to realize, the only genuine companions we shall ever have are those children of God whose very breath radiates Christ into everything we do. They become not only our companion *in* the Lord Jesus Christ, but more powerfully a companion *of* the Lord Jesus Christ.

Which is what fellowship and companionship is truly all about.

The Three Goals of Scriptural and Spirit-driven Fellowship

When we tear away the many layers of the complex subject of Scriptural fellowship, we see that fellowship, like all of Scripture, centers and relies upon the person of Jesus. And since life is about relationships, it should be no surprise to any of us that our entire lives depend upon one alive and growing relationship: becoming a *companion of Jesus Christ*.

Having companionship with another Christian is impossible without first being a companion of the King, because we can never share the fruitful fellowship with believers in the Spirit of Christ, if we are not, first and foremost, Christ's companion. And the wonderful thing is that the Lord Jesus desires us to, and asked the Father specifically for us, to be companions in unity.

"The glory which You have given Me I have given to them, that they may be one, just as We are one." –John 17:22.

One of the most heart-wrenching things to ever experience is the supreme detachment that a soul feels when it realizes that it is no longer one with the Lord, when it is no longer a companion of Christ's but, only a mere acquaintance. Scripture promises each of you that if this has happened to you Christ didn't leave you and He waits with open arms for you to seek Him again and stand at His side:

"For I am convinced that neither death, nor life, nor angels, nor principalities, nor things present, nor things to come, nor powers, nor height, nor depth, nor any other created thing, will be able to separate us from the love of God, which is in Christ Jesus our Lord." –Romans 8:31, 35, 37-39

So, we now understand that to share a like-mind with a child of God is to share the vital connection we have as children of God through the love of Jesus. Many individuals try to establish friendships with other individuals on the basis of common interests or desires or chance encounters. But I assure you that these ties will ultimately shrivel and fade because the kind of invigorating like-mindedness that we all seek can only occur through mutual faith in Jesus Christ. It is inimitably through Christ that we all share salvation, joy and love.

There are three goals that Scriptural fellowship achieves in the life of a believer that are not only essential to the Christian life, but are a blessing to companions and the entire family of God: *intimacy, unity* and *holiness*.

THE FIRST GOAL OF FELLOWSHIP: INTIMACY

Now with all this talk about true companionship and closeness this may come across to you, at first, as a suggestion to hurry out and make "companions" of everyone at your church, or work or even on the side of the street. But I assure you that that is not what I am saying at all. Let me explain.

True companionship does not normally happen among a plethora of people, but usually with a small few. You see, God made each of us in a very unique way and gifted each of us with very individual talents. And the kind of closeness and intimacy that companionship breeds is not fostered in the come and go friendships that many of us would classify as a relationship. True companionship is meant to be selective by nature because investing into the soul of another individual requires a level of vulnerability, intimacy and commitment that can never be achieved on a grand scale. Fellowship is, more often than not, God's plan for intimacy through small groups.

Just look at the New Testament and the example of discipleship and mentorship. Christ had twelve apostles. But on the night that He suffered in the Garden of Gethsemane, only three of His closest companions accompanied Him there: Peter, James and John. Paul discipled Timothy and went on missions with only one or two companions. There are and will normally only be a few people in your life who are genuine companions.

On the flip side of this, I am also not saying that you should exclude individuals from your life or dismiss people. That would also be a gross misunderstanding of what God has in mind for you. The Lord places people in your life for a reason and each of us should make every opportunity to build up another person in the Lord in any way we can.

What I am saying is not to distance yourself from everyone but a few of your closest friends, but to understand that companionship is a very special thing that will not, and does not, happen with every person you meet.

You see, Spirit-inspired fellowship often begins through the bonds of companionship but is by no means limited to that definition. Why? Because the Holy Spirit of God is not limited. I have been in a room with two people and experienced the divine presence of His love and I have also been in a Bible Conference of a hundred and fifty engrossed in His Spirit. All I know is that more often than not, two or three can genuinely gather in the name of the Lord more so than a hundred and fifty.

My aim is not to place a handcuff on what fellowship is or is not, but rather to help you understand what the Word of God reveals to us about authentic fellowship and how to apply that special blessing onto and into our daily lives. Many disciples today really have forgotten the true meaning of Christian fellowship because the word itself has taken on so many different uses in everyday "church" talk. But fellowship has a very specific meaning: fellowship hinges entirely upon the unhindered bond that Christ's followers have only through the Holy Spirit.

It is within the Holy Spirit's overflow out of our hearts that we share and deeply experience intimacy with one another because that is when we let down our guards and just come to each other as we are: fragile people who want intimacy without getting hurt. But there is a very real problem that prevents so many individuals from experiencing Scriptural and spiritual intimacy: prior painful interactions. This is no surprise to any of us as we have all probably been betrayed or hurt by individuals we let get close to us be it either talking behind our back, lying to our face or breaking our heart. Past pain always tries to smother genuine intimacy between two people because where there is intimacy there is also the great opportunity for pain to be inflicted since the very nature of intimacy is to have us with our armor and defenses down. So then who will, who can, calm our anxieties and shower us with an unshakeable trust?

Jesus Christ. The presence of the Holy Spirit protects and assures us within those times of authentic intimacy with another believer that Christ is not only "in our midst" but has become the central focus of that intimate fellowship. And since Christ is love, when Jesus becomes our very avenue of intimacy with another individual we have no need to fear:

"We have come to know and have believed the love which God has for us. God is love, and the one who abides in love abides in God, and God abides in him...There is no fear in love; but perfect love casts our fear, because fear involves punishment, and the one who fears is not perfected in love" –1 John 4 16, 18.

There is no need to fear when Christ is at the center of our connection with another child of God, when Christ holds our hands together in fellowship, because when Christ holds us together as fellow children and friends we have the very strength of God in our midst: His love.

The Second Goal of Fellowship: Unity

Our lives can not be centered upon anything other than *God the Father* because edification and love in any relationship, especially with *Jesus Christ*, is only possible through the presence and moving of the *Holy Spirit*. And within the Trinity just described we have a perfect picture of the unity and love that the Lord wants us to experience in uplifting and inspiring fellowship.

There is one particular part of Scripture that I feel expresses what the relationship between the Trinity truly is and what that means for our lives. This beautiful picture of unity and love is found in John 17: 20-26:

I […] ask […] for those […] who believe in Me […] that they may all be one; even as You, Father, are in Me and I in You, that they also may be in Us, so that the world may believe that You sent Me.

The glory which You have given Me I have given to them, that they may be one, just as We are one; I in them and You in Me, that they may be perfected in unity, so that the world may know that You sent Me, and loved them, even as You have loved Me.

Father, I desire that they also, whom You have given Me, be with Me where I am, so that they may see My glory which You have given Me, for You loved Me before the foundation of the world.

O righteous Father, although the world has not known You, Yet I have known You; and these have known that You sent Me;

and I have made Your name known to them, and will make it known, so that the love with which You loved Me may be in them, and I in them."

What I wouldn't give to have that kind of companionship and unity with anyone! Not only with my family and friends, but also with the Lord! My prayer for all of us is that the love with which the Father showered upon Christ would not only be in us, but would drip off of us onto everyone around us through the way we make His name known (there's a little appetizer for a later chapter on evangelism).

We must remember to include the Lord in our relationships on earth because if we don't, do we really have any relationships worth having at all? As you can see from these verses, the unity of Christ's disciples was so important to Jesus that He specifically asked multiple times in prayer to the Father for God's love to be in us and for Christ to always be in us, so that we may be "perfected in unity." In fact, the unity that we might attain through the love of God was so important to Jesus that He died for us, just to be with us.

True fellowship is defined in Scripture as a unity of believers, a reciprocal love shared as children of God that emerges and overflows exclusively within the presence of the Almighty. Fellowship with God the Father, God the Son and God the Spirit produces unity in the life of a believer. The perfect model for authentic fellowship and loving unity *is* the blessed Trinity.

As we have already discovered, fellowship truly hinges entirely upon the bond and unity that Christ's followers have when they are bursting at the seams with the Holy Spirit. And without the Holy Spirit of God and Christ's loving sacrifice for us, we are not a family of the Heavenly Father.

"But how can this Biblical truth be applied to my relationships with others?"

Well, because it is God's Holy Spirit that gives us the strength and mercy to help us love each other in our most darkest and selfish hour, we can take supreme confidence in the promise that our relationships with other believers do not have to be mired in gossip, pettiness, envy or heartbreak. Now do these things happen in a friendship or companionship sometimes? Unfortunately yes. Because until we get to heaven or Christ comes back to us we are all still fallen creatures and make mistakes. But it is precisely within those mistakes that the Spirit of God eagerly awaits to grant us His mercy so that we can give mercy, His wisdom so that we can know what to do and His unending love so that we can love others—no matter what!

"Above all, keep fervent in your love for one another, because love covers a multitude of sins." –1 Peter 4:8

The Third Goal of Fellowship: Holiness

A crucial part of having godly relationships that produce true fellowship is to understand one very important thing: to have a godly relationship you must make it a God-relationship. Too many times we neglect the Lord in our friendships by the way we talk to our friends or about our friends to others.

For the longest time I had a best friend, who was also a Christian, but we never talked about the Lord. Can you believe that? "How could he have been your best friend then, based on your definition of fellowship and companionship?" That's a good question. For the years that I knew him and spent time hanging out with him, because our relationship was not based on Christ and didn't really include Christ by the way we spoke or acted around each other, he wasn't my best friend. But even more troubling to me is the reality that Christ wasn't my best friend during that time either.

So how did we become best friends in Christ? How can any of us escape an ultimately fractured and fallen friendship? Well, as the devotion chapter showed us, sometimes pain is the only way that we will ever listen to the Lord. My friend suffered a tragic loss in his life and sought my council and company for comfort and support. Out of that event he and I prayed our way into an authentic friendship and have since lived our lives through a Spirit-filled companionship. We are not only able to talk about the Lord now and worship Him together, but we look forward to it.

Now does everyone escape a fallen friendship this way? No. The best way to escape a fallen friendship is to attack the problem head on and discuss with that friend what must stop and what must start. Many times this leads to the loss of a friendship because many individuals don't want to sacrifice vulgarities and ungodly rhetoric for a fulfilling and edifying companionship. But rest assured in the knowledge that that individual was never really your friend in the first place. Friendship and companionship are not built on conditions, but on commitment, on compassion, on Christ.

The worst thing you can do is to jeopardize your companionship with

Christ for the sinful friendship of another by neglecting the Lord in that friendship. You see, the Holy Spirit can't empower you into true fellowship when you exclude Him from your relationships, from your life. Holiness is the domain of the Holy Spirit. To live outside that domain is to prohibit the entrance of Christ into your relationships, not to mention life.

The second worst thing you can do is to neglect the company of a friend in Christ because you're neglecting the Lord. You may prohibit the Holy Spirit from truly guiding your heart and life, but companions who are overflowing with the Holy Spirit will not be kept at bay because the Holy Spirit will not be kept at bay from a child of God no matter how far they have strayed. Spirit-driven fellowship means we are all to be held accountable for our relationships with the Lord, *especially* when we don't want to be. Therein lies the beauty of genuine fellowship: someone is always there to love us, help us and empower us.

So what would happen if we truly lived our lives in Spirit-empowering fellowship? Well, by basing our gatherings, services and relationships on bringing His presence into our lives we would rekindle the flame of passionate adoration for the Lord that seems waning in our daily encounters. And by doing so we not only would love one another in holiness, but we would love God through our love for each other.

By understanding the necessity for every child of God to be linked daily in a vibrant relationship with the Father, Son and Holy Spirit, we can all begin to edify one another, forgive one another and genuinely fellowship with each other because we will all be relying not upon our own abilities to produce and maintain fulfilling relationships, but we would be completely dependent upon the only source that nourishes relationships: *the presence of God*.

Application:

Don't forget about Jesus!

I know that statement pretty much sums up the entire effort of Christianity as a whole (and honestly how could any of us forget about our Lord), but this is an especially difficult thing to accomplish in our *daily* relationships. But often we do forget about our Lord, not permanently, yet in the way that we put others before Him in our daily lives.

First and foremost, Christ is meant to not only be your Lord and Savior, but your constant companion and friend. And what an honor and privilege it is, no matter how undeserving, to be a friend of the King. Not only do we neglect our friendship with Christ on a daily basis, but we neglect His presence in our friendships with others by basing our friendships with other people on ungodly things. We don't realize it, but if our friendships do not glorify the Lord, then they're demeaning Him instead.

So how can we start glorifying Him in our friendships and stop excluding Christ?

Well, an example of this could be that if you do not feel that what you're discussing is particularly appealing or inviting to the Holy Spirit of God in conversations, stop discussing whatever it is you're discussing with your friend, friends or colleagues.

This application basically centers around all of us trying to keep Jesus Christ as our first companion, which is impossible if we place having fun with one of our friends above keeping the Holy Spirit of God in our midst.

In the end, we must all ask ourselves, "Do we serve man—or God?"

Prayer:

Most Holy and Loving Father God we thank You that You loved us in Christ so much that You sent Your only Son to die for us, so that we could abide in You. May we never take for granted just how much You sacrificed so that we could be with You forever! I ask that You bless us with the heart of unity and fellowship that You have in the midst of the Trinity, Lord. And even though we may never understand Your fellowship or Your Trinity God, help us to live our lives in the presence of Your Spirit so that we may have companionship with our brothers and sisters here like You have with the Son and the Spirit, Father. Grant us the wisdom and mercy to lift each other up and edify each other in Your Spirit so that we might all become a family of God! But most importantly, Lord, may we never distance ourselves from being constantly and intimately Your companion in all that we do and are. Thank You for loving us and grant us the strength to be a companion of Christ. In the precious name of Jesus and for His sake always, Amen.

Chapter Eleven

And the Greatest of These Is: Love

"A new commandment I give to you, that you love one another, even as I have loved you, that you also love one another. By this all men will know that you are My disciples, if you have love for one another...If you love Me, you will keep My commandments."
—Jesus of Nazareth

"Little children, let us not love with word or with tongue, but in deed and truth...We have come to know and have believed the love which God has for us. God is love, and the one who abides in love abides in God, and God abides in him...We love, because He first loved us."
—John the Beloved

PANG!

PUNG!

PING!

Are any of you familiar with these sounds? When I was a small child I absolutely could not pry myself away from kitchenware, specifically the pleasing sound that banging pots and pans together makes, much to the chagrin of my mother. I cherished the ringing of the aluminum throughout our small kitchen and even though the crash would sometimes startle me, I would slam the bottoms of the pots together even louder with wide eyes and reckless glee.

Now to my mother (or any other human around me most likely), I'm sure that the clang and pop of metal colliding with metal sounded only like clatter. But what would have happened if my small hands had moved with a unified purpose in striking those pans? What would have happened if I intentionally hit the pots at specific moments and then didn't hit them at others? The clamor would have begun to resemble a rhythmic drumming. In fact, the displeasure of metal scraping metal would have been transformed into the beautiful melody of music. Instead of just banging the pots together without motivation, I would have been playing the pans like a musical instrument in a symphony.

Sound would have shifted from noise to harmony. Our lives are the same when it comes to love. We are either moved by love with a unified purpose or we are devoid of love and move aimlessly about life. Without love as the motivating spark in our life and actions, every deed we perform is just making noise. We will be Paul's noisy gong or clanging symbol in 1 Corinthians 13 because we will be one instrument playing out of tune, the tune of God's love for us through Christ.

A lot of people think that love is either some chemical that our brain produces or is a sort of destiny that is produced when we meet the perfect mate, but that is not what love really is at all. Love does not occur out of random chance synapses in our mind or out of a scripted, sentimental encounter, but is only ignited by Almighty God. Without a sincere and complete devotion to loving Christ we can never achieve any harmony with His will and His grace because we will not be doing anything through Him or of Him: God is love.

There is no doubt that out of every other thing in this existence, we can never comprehend the fullness and true intricacies of love. Why? Because God is love, love is God, and since we can never fully grasp with our limited understanding what God is, then there is *no* chance for us to fully grasp love. However, the Lord Jesus Christ has given us the best definition and description of love: *Himself.* We need only Jesus to see the truth behind love (when it comes to seeing any truth really) because everything starts and ends with Jesus the Christ. Take, for example, the desire that each of us feels to be loved unconditionally.

At the very core of our human frailty and basic desires is one thing: we all just want someone to care. We want someone who is going to do more than simply ask us, "how are you doing today?" and then walk away as if our response didn't matter as much as their asking the question. We want to be able to be loved by someone despite our shortcomings and flaws. In essence, we want to be loved despite being unlovable.

And yet, we can *never* find this love in its ultimate perfection unless we turn our eyes upon the cross of our Lord Jesus Christ. Unless we turn to God with this fundamental need, we will be "striving after wind" in the midst of the Lord's love-hurricane. We will be searching for something to dampen us when we are constantly being showered every moment. God's love is always beaming down onto all of us throughout our lives. Remember, the best definition of love and *how to* love is found only in Christ.

So, how do we turn to God with this love-need? How can we offer up to a Perfect Loving Being our grossly inadequate form of love if He is its author? How do we become creatures of love and not apathy? The old saying is right, "the opposite of love is not hate; it is apathy." However, I believe that at the center of this quote lies the greatest definition of love and hate.

The opposite of love, which entails loving God and those around you, is not simply emotional hate or feeling anger and enmity towards God and those around you. No, the true polarized version of love is the greatest danger a human soul can face: *Not feeling anything at all towards God or those around you.*

Hate is just a momentary emotion. Apathy is a way of living. Therefore, one can say that apathy is the truest definition of condemnation towards God and your neighbor. Not feeling any emotion or response is the grossest and sincerest form of rejection because to not feel anything is to have completely hardened your heart to the call of Christ.

Or to put in simpler terms, choosing to disregard and not to care anything about God or your fellow man is choosing yourself over your Maker and your neighbors in every way. And this way of self-centered existence is anti-Christ. Because Christ was not self-centered, He was God-centered. He was eternally others-centered.

Now don't immediately panic and think that I am saying everyone who grows frustrated will be sent to hell and is a liar. Feeling upset towards your family member who pointed out your pimple in front of your friends or colleagues does not equal hating your brother (neighbor). However, if your life is characterized by a negativity and anger towards everyone and everything around you, then maybe you might need to reassess your ability to love a perfect God, let alone other flawed people.

> "If someone says 'I love God,' and yet hates his brother, he is a liar; for the one who does not love his brother whom he has seen, cannot love God whom he has not seen. And this commandment we have from Him, that the one who loves God should love his brother also." *–1 John 4:20-21.*

Upon living a life of apathy, the process of you being dragged down into the abyss has already begun. We must remember that hell is the complete and total absence of God, of love. I fear that there are many people today who have one foot already in hell spiritually and emotionally as they walk with both feet atop this earth. Can someone who does this be a child of God?

Nope. Not according to the Word of God. As voiced by 1 John, we have been given a commandment, a necessity of action in this lifetime, if we really love God. The commandment we have been handed is to love the Lord our God with every fiber of our being and to love each other as He loved us, as we would love ourselves: unconditionally.

But if we do not understand what the real definition of love is, if we do not understand how we can love or even how to go about loving, then how can we ever fulfill the greatest commandment?

The Two Essential Truths that Lead to a Life of Love

I believe that there are two essential truths to living a life of love. And if we do not or are not partaking in these truths daily, then we are not really loving anyone, and have become incapable of loving like the Father does.

The first essential truth is that love is a committed decision to be like God towards Him and His creations (others around us); *love is an attitude expressed in actions*. And the second essential truth is that authentic, powerful love is found in complete dependence upon and devotion to Christ; *love is laying down your life every day to the Lord Jesus*.

LOVE IS A COMMITTED DECISION TO BE LIKE GOD; ATTITUDES EXPRESSED IN ACTIONS.

As stated earlier, love is not romance or an ideology about constant feelings of infatuation and fluttering hearts. Love is a sacrifice, an action, a state of being. It is not about liking someone or even enjoying their company at times, but about treating them in a manner in which you would wish others would always treat your child, your dearest loved one—or yourself.

Love is a decision, a choice you make daily, just like believing is. Many, many people turn away from Christianity because of the impossibilities (they think) that lie within the words, "Love your enemies" or "Love your neighbor as yourself." Why? Because this commandment is seen as forcing or falsifying feelings and thus seems not only completely ludicrous and absurd, but impossible.

There is no way it is humanly possible to love someone you despise or who has just committed atrocities against your best friend, family member or…Savior….is there? No, they are completely correct. There is no *humanly* possible way to do it. But thank God we don't depend upon our own humanity for salvation and joy! There may be no human way to do it, but there is God's way.

Once again, the source of this conflict rises out of our fleshly habits of relying or only focusing upon our own limited abilities or power: a.k.a pride. So why, once again, does humility pop up when discussing the love of others through God's eyes and Son? Well despite humility being, perhaps, the largest requirement of faith, hope and love in God, there is a specific answer for why humility pertains to love.

Real love is the humility we discussed previously in its *purest* form. It is to be eternally thinking of someone else's good, wishing the best for them, hoping they become the godly man or woman you know that God wills them to be and during this entire process, never giving a single thought or consideration to yourself. Real love is to lose yourself (your "self") in the love of someone else.

Now I do not mean emotions or passion, although these can be some of the most tangible and strongest forms of authentic love. Those are fleeting and temporary, but the other, deeper and unseen forms of authentic love never fade and never "fail," as Paul so eloquently said in 1 Corinthians 13.

To forget about our "selves" is to fully love God and those around us, because our sight is not blinded by fleshly, egocentric vision. And then we become like our Savior; we begin to emulate His very existence. The true nature of living a life of love does not occur naturally to us at all as we try to emulate the Lord's life through our own. Brennan Manning sums up just what loving like Jesus takes in His devotional book, *Reflections for Ragamuffins:*

> Our natural repugnance and ingrained resistance to the inconvenient, unpleasant, and often messy business of compassionate caring is well illustrated by a story told at a recent AA meeting: A construction worker stopped after work for a few beers at the local watering hole and got home just in time for dinner.
>
> His little daughter, who had peanut butter and jelly all over her face as well as a deposit in her pants, rushed into his arms. To say that he was "taken aback" would not accurately describe his emotional state. Wheeling around to his wife, he muttered, 'How the hell do you love something that smells like this?'
>
> Calmly she replied, 'In the same way I love a husband who comes home stinking drunk and amorous. You work at it. [39]

You can't "love your neighbor as yourself" if you base that love on them being attractive, or kind, or a delight to be around. I think this is why so many people harbor such disbelief when it comes to love as a practice and not as a theory because the expectation that God has of us is quite drastic. Or, it at least appears that way at first glance.

But upon a further inspection of His commandment, we can see that love, like any other spiritual discipline, really does come down to having to work at it. Always having a heart towards love is as foreign to us as walking on water, but Christ called Peter out onto the waves nonetheless. So, we better establish our focus now solely on Christ, like Peter did as he stepped out of the boat, and prepare to get our feet wet.

Because if we find it difficult to love the "neighbor" who slightly annoys us by always having one more thing than you do, what will become of our life of love when we are called to love our enemies—which we are. C.S. Lewis describes this monumental struggle against our selves and for the sake of Christ:

> We must try to feel about the enemy as we feel about ourselves—to wish that he were not bad, to hope that he may, in this world or another,

be cured: in fact, to wish his good. That is what is meant in the Bible by loving him: wishing his good, not feeling fond of him nor saying he is nice when he is not.

I admit that this means loving people who have nothing loveable about them. But then, has oneself anything lovable about it? You love it simply because it is yourself. God intends us to love all selves in the same way and for the same reason: but He has given us the sum [already] worked out in our own case to show us how it works.

We have then to go on and apply the rule to all the other selves. Perhaps it makes it easier if we remember that is how He loves us. Not for any nice, attractive qualities we think we have, but just because we are the things called selves [His creation]. For there really is nothing else in us to love. [40]

At first glance, loving your enemies and neighbors seems like a quaint, "warm-fuzzy" concept to "always be extremely fond and happy with all of the people around you and to never feel animosity or anger or fight," as Lewis stated. But loving anyone, let alone an enemy, is as much a struggle as trying to blink away those pesky dots you see when your eyes linger too long on the sun: sometimes—it just takes time and a lot of patience for your focus to regain clarity.

That being said, we need to really get a crystal definition of what love truly is and is not, as it applies to our life.

Love is not feeling fond of someone no matter what they do.

If we were always extremely fond and happy with all of the people around us at all times, which would include the moments they sinned against God and tried to harm us, we would be disobeying the Word of God and therefore falling into sin ourselves. And since God is love and can not be anywhere near sin we would not be truly loving if we always felt affection towards everybody, no matter what they did.

So if we don't exactly appreciate an individual at a given moment, our act of love is not to try and manufacture those fuzzy feelings for them, but to treat them as though we did appreciate them and hope that they will always find appreciation and love.

Love is not letting your heart or life be trampled

Loving someone does not mean allowing them to walk all over you or to never fight back, because sometimes when you do not fight, which does include fighting for your God, then you are in sin (see some of the history of Israel in the Old Testament).

Now many are martyred for the cause of Christ and many lose their lives for the kingdom of God. I am not discounting suffering persecution or trying not to sin by abstaining from violent acts as a glorification of the

Lord, I am simply stating the fact that passivity is not the all and all answer to every situation; seeking Christ is. In the same way an abused wife should not subject herself to the abuse of her husband through passivity, the children of God can not be silent as God is slandered, Christ is mocked, and our brothers and sisters in Christ suffer.

"Do not withhold good from those to whom it is due, when it is in your power to do it." –Proverbs 3:27

The Good Samaritan parable echoes this Scriptural truth, as does Galatians 6:9-10:

"Let us not lose heart in doing good, for in due time we will reap if we do not grow weary. So then, while we have opportunity let us do good to all people, and especially to those who are of the household of the faith."

Love is action, not inaction. Love is something you do, not something you don't do. With a clear and Scriptural view of what love truly is, we can begin to learn how we should pursue a life of love: *sincerely for Christ*.

SECONDLY, LOVE IS LAYING DOWN YOUR LIFE TO CHRIST DAILY; DOING THE SPIRITUAL DISCIPLINES OUT OF LOVE FOR JESUS AND NOTHING ELSE

The importance of being devoted only to Christ (as discussed in previous chapters) is that our only hope to love the Lord our God with our utmost being and love our neighbors as we love ourselves is through the growth a believer experiences when they are vitally connected to the Holy Spirit in their daily life: becoming more like Christ. Because being totally devoted to the Lord Jesus is our only hope to becoming more like Him.

In essence, every chapter up until now has been a way, a path, in which you can take to do just that, to crucify yourself daily and live in Christ. But if you pursue any and all of these spiritual disciplines and take these paths without love and sincerity, they are meaningless and useless. Oswald Chambers thoroughly examines what it means to be devoted to Christ and how to lay one's life down for Him in His classic work, *My Utmost for His Highest:*

> If I am a friend of Jesus, I must deliberately and carefully lay down my life for Him.
>
> It is a difficult thing to do, and thank God that it is. Salvation is easy for us, because it cost God so much. But the exhibiting of salvation in my life is difficult. God saves a person, fills him with the Holy Spirit, and then says, in effect, 'Now you work it out in your life, and be faithful to Me, even though the nature of everything around you is to cause you to be unfaithful. –June 16 [41]

The most difficult thing about walking with Christ is the day to day surrendering of our hopes, dreams, aspirations and desires in order to conform to the image of Christ. It almost sounds cruel on God's part but oh, how it is not! To become like Christ is to become love itself. It is to become joy in the midst of suffering and pain. It is to become light in a world of darkness.

"But how do we *lovingly* and *sincerely* surrender ourselves daily to Christ? Seriously, how can we apply this somewhat distant idea to a real-life application?"

Simply put, we must keep Christ where He belongs: at the very top. We must love the Lord Jesus with all of our hearts, minds, souls and strength; we must keep Him as our treasure.

"Where your treasure is, there your heart will be also." –Matthew 6:21.

To become more like Christ we must keep Him as our original love and then love Him like He is above everything else in our lives. A treasure demands all of an individual's attention, focus and heart as Scripture tells us. Whatever an individual holds closest to their heart is what overflows into their daily life and actions. We will only be filled with enough of Christ's love to authentically love others as He did, *selflessly*, when He is the one thing we hold closest to our heart.

Love, in any relationship or concrete sense of the word, is never about gaining or experiencing some intangible concept or feeling, but rather a decision to offer all of yourself to someone else so that they may not only love you in return, but so that you can grow in their love. Only then, when you have emptied yourself of your fear of vulnerability and disappointment, will you be open to receiving anything. To receive anything from Jesus, likewise, we must give Him everything.

But sometimes in order for us to have Christ as our first love means we must take something or someone else out of the top spot—including ourselves. I believe that one of the saddest events today is the desire that many professing Christians have to put the stamp of "Jesus" onto their own personal desires or interests. I can think of many pastors, authors and televangelists who are more concerned with their own "words" than the Living Word of God: Jesus Christ.

Chambers saw the importance of correcting this fatal error in the life of a child of the King by concluding that:

"The fountains from which love flows are in God, not in us. It is absurd to think that the love of God is naturally in our hearts, as a result of our own nature. His love is there only because it "has been poured out in our hearts by the Holy Spirit" [...] The life of God exhibits itself in this spontaneous way because the fountains of His love are in the Holy Spirit." –April 30 [42]

Our only chance for loving God and each other is the moving of the Holy Spirit within us. This constant work of the Holy Spirit in our lives, the reciprocal love of God between Christ and each of us is the "feeding of His sheep" that Christ calls each of us to do. As the old saying goes, "actions speak louder than words." Telling someone you love Jesus is cheap when compared to someone actually knowing and feeling that you love Jesus through your very presence and life, which is more powerful than any word you can utter or deed you can do.

It is this love that shines through the darkness. It is this love that consumes and burns each of us into a passionate devotion to our Savior. Have you ever been around someone who is completely devoted and in love with the Lord Jesus Christ? What was the result in your heart, your mind, your soul?

In my experiences, whenever I have been around an individual who is utterly in love with the Lord and therefore can't help but love the people they see, the result is quite heavenly. And when that individual leaves I soon come to the realization that I still have a lot of work to do…so I'd better get started.

We have been passionately called to love. The only chance for love in any way, shape or form is through laying down our lives before Christ and sacrificing ourselves for His will. And through this unshakeable devotion the love of God's Holy Spirit pours out from our hearts and lives into the lives and hearts of others, accomplishing the most extraordinary thing: becoming more like Christ and less like ourselves.

Application:

Truly lay down your life to Jesus Christ this week. If you have never done it before I urge you to accept the gift of God's love: accept Christ as your Lord and Savior. If you have, make a deliberate effort to lay down your life in every aspect of your week to Him. Truly love Him daily by keeping Him as your first and only love, since all love that you might show to anyone else must first and foremost come from the love of God.

Secondly, love your neighbor. Instead of being quick to judge or abrupt (short) with an individual (outwardly through your actions or secretly in your heart), truly make a decision to hope for their best, to show them courtesy and compassion. This does not mean accept their bad actions or sin. It means accept them unconditionally as God does you. It means being really patient.

Also, try to go out of your way to let others know that Christ loves them. I had a friend who was going through a horrible time, which I was unaware of at the time, but for some odd reason one day I felt compelled to tell her that Jesus loves her. She stood there with wide eyes and a dropped jaw until her eyes began to fill with tears.

We just looked at each other for a moment.

She then slowly nodded with a knowing smile and said, "Thank you."

Sometimes, we all need to be reminded of the love He has for us; usually by His children showing us His love in words, but also, mainly, in action.

Love everyone as Christ loves you: just as you are.

Prayer:

Thank You Heavenly Father for the unfathomable love that You have for every single one of us. Thank You for Jesus Christ, the expression of Your loving kindness to us, our Lord and Savior. Help us to love You more, Father. Help us to love each other and those who do not know You more completely. We ask You to fill us up with Your sovereign Holy Spirit so that Your love may not only pour out of us, but touch and transform not only our lives but the lives of those around us. May we never use the name of Jesus for anything but in our complete devotion and love to Him. May we always remember You and continue to love You with all of our heart, mind, soul and strength and love our neighbors as ourselves and love all as You have loved us. Please help us to love more like Your Son Jesus Christ and less like ourselves. In Jesus Name always. Amen.

Chapter Twelve

Go: Evangelism

> *"Go therefore and make disciples of all nations, baptizing them in the name of the Father and the Son and the Holy Spirit, teaching them to observe all that I commanded you; and lo, I am with you always, even to the end of the age."*
> —Jesus of Nazareth

> *"Then the Spirit said to Philip, 'Go up and join this chariot.' Philip ran up and heard him [the Ethiopian] reading Isaiah the prophet, and said, 'Do you understand what you are reading?' And [the Ethiopian] said, 'Well, how could I, unless someone guides me?'"*
> —The Acts of the Apostles

How did you come to know Christ? I want you to honestly try and remember that day and more specifically, the process of how your salvation happened. Because odds are you did not come to know the Lord Jesus completely on your own; someone helped you. Someone shared with you the love and hope of Jesus Christ.

And it is that, my friends, my brothers and sisters, which the Lord commissions all of us to do. He does not assign us to go and pound Scripture and doctrine down a person's throat or overly condemn them with hellfire and brimstone. The majority of people in this world already know they are in need of love and hope, as we all hear the Voice calling us to come and be filled. We all hurt and long for peace and happiness.

And it is within this weary and burdened heart that the Lord Jesus sends us out as witnesses to the ends of the earth. We go out as physicians for the wounded, not torturers of the condemned. Every single follower of Christ has been charged with the simple goal of giving everyone they come in contact with one thing: the Answer they're looking for. The Answer we have found.

Evangelism at its very core is a personal testimony about what Jesus has done in your life and what He can do in the lives of the people you share your story with every day. Spreading the Gospel is not an opportunity for us to flaunt our intellectual acumen or mercilessly disprove others in their wrong ideas or beliefs. Not at all! When we tell others about Jesus we end up doing precisely what Christ did for every single human being He ever came into contact with while He walked this earth. No matter who approached Jesus with a hungry heart and a seeking soul, He gave them all what we are called to give them through the sharing of our faith: the comfort and hope they desperately need.

There is a reason this chapter follows the chapter on love. Evangelism is not a part of Christianity that only some "gifted" believers are able to do. We, all of us who profess belief in Jesus Christ, are called to spread the gospel to the ends of the earth. In fact, an eagerness to tell another about the love you've found and have in Christ is usually the best indicator of a person who is serious about becoming more like Christ.

The Great Commission is a commandment from the Lord that is saturated with His love for a weary and suffering world. The story of Christ itself is a story of love. And everyone who ever takes in a breath on this planet frantically yearns to be loved. The reason Christ calls all of us to be His witnesses is the simple fact that He has already loved us and because of that, we have been given the gift that everyone else longs to receive. And that is why it is our privilege and our utmost responsibility to share that gift, the greatest gift we can ever receive, with every single person we lay eyes on.

So why don't we? What prevents us from unabashedly sharing what Christ has given us with people we know are hurting and hoping to be loved? Simply put, we must not see sharing the gospel with others as spreading the love of Christ. We see it as putting ourselves into an uncomfortable situation and placing our "respectability" or "stature" at risk. How many of us do not speak up that we are Christians when we know we should? How many of us act ashamed of the glorious gospel of Christ when the Holy Spirit of God burns in us to speak up and shed our insecurity for the power of God? Do any of us reveal or live by the one thing that grants us eternal life: our faith?

"For I am not ashamed of the gospel, for it is the power of God for salvation to everyone who believes, to the Jew first and also to the Greek. For in it the righteousness of God is revealed from faith to faith; as it is written, 'But the righteous man shall live by faith" –Romans 1: 16-17.

I love the first line of Romans 1:16-17! We must not be ashamed of the gospel! For we all know and believe, we must if we call ourselves children of God, that the gospel is the very power of God. The gospel, the story of Jesus, is salvation to everyone who believes. But many of us, too many times myself included, do act ashamed of the gospel when in the presence of those who disregard and even disparage the Good News.

And while we sit there or stand there silent, in the midst of a God-given opportunity to share how the love of Christ has changed us, we forget one very powerful promise that Jesus also gave us. "I am with you always." How could we ever forget that? How could that, of all things, slip away? But we do forget.

We forget that He is with us always, whispering to us the words of love and grace that the hurting hearts in this lost world need to hear. And most important of all we forget that it is He who speaks to their hearts and not us. We are not trying to sell them or solicit them some sales pitch. We are letting Jesus do the talking and more importantly the healing.

It just so happens that He has chosen to speak and work through us. So why don't we give Him every opportunity to tell the beauty of His story?

The Two Effects Evangelism Has on Burdened, Weary People

Evangelism or reaching out to others with the message of Jesus Christ impacts people on such a powerfully personal level that the healing effects can not be overlooked. Sharing the love that Christ has blessed you with and the peace you have and will have for all eternity has two effects on burdened, weary hearts: *Evangelism helps lost and hurting people find the Answer they're searching for* and *evangelism plants the seeds of His truth and peace; lays the kindling for the spark of God's consuming fire.*

First Effect: Evangelism helps lost and hurting people find the Answer they're searching for

How many of us really look at sharing the message of salvation as a chance to heal the broken-hearted soul who has wandered away from the true Shepherd? I know I didn't for the longest time. And then one day I was asked to share my testimony in a lesson for a church group and as I began to outline my life before coming to Christ, which is an essential part to your testimony and evangelism, I suddenly came to a realization that I had never seen before. It was only upon deep reflection of my testimony and the life I lived before I came to Christ that my perspective on evangelism changed forever.

Below are the notes that I scribbled together during this moment of new found memory:

"I don't remember hopelessness, fear of hell or emptiness during the seconds of my conversion from my old life into the new, everlasting one, but I do remember Christ in every single moment that passed me by; all He is and all I am not, all I love and all He gives, all I want and all He has done.

And now, as I sit here, I imagine the profound weakness that existing would be without Him—and that moves me to love those who do not know Him and do not believe in Him. Because that is what they are without God. They are not inferior, more evil or more wretched than I. Not at all. The lost are a sunset without colors, seen only through grey, a shadow of what could be that is filled only with fear and despair.

Because when it comes down to it, when I look at this life of mine in complete and brutal honesty, I know within every part of my being that the only difference between the unbelieving world and myself—is the grace of God.

And that compels me to not turn my eyes, my back and my heart from others. For what is a sunset without gold, without blue, without prismatic splendor? What is a body without a heart? What is a child without their parent? What is a man or woman without their God? What is a soul without Christ? The answer: nothing.

So how can I stay silent? How can I keep my mouth closed and my heart cold with the knowledge of such utter and desperate need? I can't. I mustn't. And most importantly: I won't. I refuse to leave others where I once was: alone and lost. I will follow Jesus.

I *will* tell the world!

Even now those scribbled words send shivers up my spine. I get chills because the focus is so clear, it's all so simple. If only the focus was always that clear. We tell the world because we can't live with the thought that the world is currently how we once were—hopeless. We can't live with the knowledge that others can't live, now and forever, without the saving grace of Christ!

And I can't emphasize the words "saving grace" enough. We don't share the gospel to promote doctrines or dogmas. We tell others about Jesus so that they will no longer be a shell of the person God wishes them to be. We offer the message of Christ so that that person might receive eternal life. We speak His words so that they will never be alone again.

If we look at Acts chapter 8 we will see that a searching person still needs help from a genuine guide:

"Then the Spirit said to Philip, 'Go up and join this chariot.'

Philip ran up and heard him [the Ethiopian eunuch] reading Isaiah the prophet, and said, 'Do you understand what you are reading?'

And [the Ethiopian] said, 'Well how could I, unless someone guides me?' And he invited Philip to come up and sit with him...

Then Philip opened his mouth, and preached Jesus to him. As they went along the road they came to some water; and the eunuch said, 'Look! Water! What prevents me from being baptized?'

And Philip said, 'If you believe with all your heart, you may.' And he answered and said, 'I believe that Jesus Christ is the Son of God.' And [the Ethiopian] ordered the chariot to stop; and they both went down into the water, Philip as well as the eunuch, and [Philip] baptized him." –Acts 8: 29-31, 35-37

I find it especially poignant that the Ethiopian's answer to a question about understanding the Word of God was itself, a question, "Well how could I, unless someone guides me?" Questions are all that the soul without the Holy Spirit has; relentless, tormenting questions. But the Holy Spirit is the Guide within each of us that we have been blessed with in order to help the inquirer find the Answer. We must never forget that we are *not* the Guide, but a fellow wanderer who has been found.

If we were to continually treat the lost in this way, as we are no different than they are except for the saving mercy of the Lord, perhaps we would care for them more as people who desperately need a savior, whether they consciously realize it or not. And maybe if we did, we would care more about them finding the salvation and peace within the words of the Lord's than focusing on making sure we speak the right ones.

The lost sheep, which is how Christ refers to those who do not know Him, do not want to hear about complex doctrines or theological concepts when they *first* hunger for fulfillment; they long for food. They long for the Bread of Life, the redemption and nourishment that can only be found in Christ Jesus.

How can any of us withhold food from a starving, wayward soul?

SECOND EFFECT: EVANGELISM HELPS PLANT THE SEEDS OF HIS TRUTH AND PEACE; LAYING THE KINDLING FOR THE SPARK OF GOD'S CONSUMING FIRE.

> "The duty of a faithful missionary is to concentrate on keeping his soul completely and continually open to the nature of the Lord Jesus Christ. The men and women our Lord sends out on His endeavors are ordinary human people, but people who are controlled by their devotion to Him, which has been brought about through the work of the Holy Spirit."
> –Oswald Chambers, *My Utmost for His Highest*, October 18 [43]

Missionaries are you and me; the followers of Christ. They are not only the people who go overseas and learn new languages in strange, faraway lands; a missionary is already a child of God in a foreign land. So guess what, that describes every single believer in Christ because we are all adopted children of God who live in a foreign, fallen world.

The man or woman who works near an individual who does not know Christ is a missionary. The schoolteacher who instructs a boy or girl who doesn't know Christ is a missionary. This means that we are missionaries no matter what our vocation or situation happens to be. We are called to be an example of the Lord Jesus (which is evangelism as well) and we are called to live a life in Christ so that His Holy fire would send sparks off of us onto the unbelieving world around us.

So how does this happen? Well first off: practice what you preach. If you give someone a long spiel about how important it is to love and show mercy to your neighbor and then you scream at the person across the street because their trash blew into your yard, guess what, you've just doused yourself and them in the muck of hypocrisy. The greatest threat to anyone's ability to share the Good News of what Christ has done in their life is the glaring inconsistencies between what they say and what they do.

Now does this mean you will never mess up? Of course not, you're human. But does that mean you can just do whatever you want without thinking about what the consequences of your actions are for the sake of Christ? Never! In fact if you're a believer, you must realize that the unbelieving world holds you under a billion-magnification microscope.

And though the children of God have all of this pressure on their shoulders, remember that our focus is solely on Christ and not on ourselves. Remove that yoke from around your neck about impressing people. Because if we are only concerned with impressing people, we will certainly not be devoted to impressing God. We shed our burdens and receive the yoke, the tutelage of Christ, so that we might please our Father.

And after all, which one will bring others to Christ: impressing the fallen or impressing the Divine, who breathes flames of penitence onto the frozen hearts of man? It's not about impressing men but keeping our focus and souls in an intertwined state with the heart and Spirit of God.

Second, you must understand that you have work to do. All of us have a very specific job to do every single day and that is to show others the Lord Jesus Christ. God did not say occasionally spread the gospel or only preach and teach the Word on Sundays. No, He commissioned us to be missionaries always because He is with us always as Scripture tells us:

> "But sanctify Christ as Lord in your hearts, always *being* ready to make a defense to everyone who asks you to give an account for the hope that is in you, yet with gentleness and reverence." –1 Peter 3:15

> "Go therefore and make disciples of all nations, baptizing them in the name of the Father and the Son and the Holy Spirit, teaching them to observe all that I commanded you; and lo, I am with you always, even to the end of the age" –Matthew 28: 19-20

If we don't live and breathe the Word of God and glorify the truth of His sovereign majesty—no one will! We all have a job to do and the Lord has given us the perfect equipment to handle the task: His Holy Spirit. In the Gospel of John chapters 14 and 16, Jesus blesses each of us with an exhilarating message on just how helpful the Helper and Spirit of truth, truly is:

> "I will ask the Father, and He will give you another Helper, that He may be with you forever; that is the Spirit of truth, whom the world cannot

receive, because it does not see Him or know Him, but you know Him because He abides with you and will be in you.

I will not leave you as orphans; I will come to you [...]

But the Helper, the Holy Spirit, whom the Father will send in My name, He will teach you all things, and bring to your remembrance all that I said to you

[...]

And He, when He comes, will convict the world concerning sin and righteousness and judgment; concerning sin, because they do not believe in Me; and concerning righteousness, because I go to the Father and you no longer see Me [...]

But when He, the Spirit of truth, comes, He will guide you into all the truth; for He will not speak on His own initiative, but whatever He hears, He will speak; and He will disclose to you what is to come.

He will glorify Me, for He will take of Mine and will disclose it to you."

Anytime I feel inadequate about my stuttering problem, (and if any one of you reading this could hear me try and say Mississippi you'd think someone shoved a rotating sprinkler head into my mouth), anytime I feel self-conscious about it before I talk to someone about Christ that verse always eases my angst. I mean what do we have to fear if Christ Himself will disclose to us what to say and the Spirit of God will do the convicting for us?

I wonder if that is why so many people are so easily turned away by messages centering on the awfulness of sin. Perhaps they've already heard that from the Holy Spirit of God and we are just repeating the same thing to them over and over again, like a song on the radio that just never seems to stop playing, without including the good part of the song.

In my experiences with people who are *seeking* the Lord, they have no problems realizing that they are sinners. Their biggest problem is realizing He is God and loves them, desires them to be His child *despite* their sin. In fact, the biggest question I'm ever confronted with, by people who don't even know I'm a Christian is the same one Pontius Pilate asked Jesus:

"What is truth?" –John 18:38.

If a person asks you this question in one form or another, they do not need to hear (*initially*) how wrong they are in what they believe or how awful of a person they are for believing in whatever it is they believe in. I think that is a craft of the devil to try and distract us from allowing the Spirit of God to actually and authentically answer their question, and more specifically, their need.

When a person comes to you seeking truth, give them the Truth, not cold condemnation. Don't give them hatred or reckless rebuke. Just give them the Eternal Truth: Jesus.

"For this I have been born, and for this I have come into the world, to testify to the truth. Everyone who is of the truth hears My voice" –John 18:37.

You'll be amazed at how open an individual will be to listening to what you believe when you give them exactly what they're lacking and longing for: faith. Once you have shared the message of how Christ changed your life and showed you true love, no matter how dark and damp the state of their heart is before the Lord, you lay dry kindling throughout their soul.

And then, maybe years down the line, they will experience something or meet someone that will provide a tiny spark to that dry kindling (if you have not ignited it already). And then the encircling smoke of His Holy Spirit will fill their thoughts and suddenly a single flame of passion and devotion will ignite inside their being.

All of us have that fire inside of us if we are brothers and sisters in Christ because the Holy Spirit's flame can not be doused or conquered by anyone or anything; no, the Spirit consumes us. So then all it takes on our part is a few words about the love and life of Jesus to spark a wildfire of salvation to sweep across the land!

Application:

Remember how you came to Christ. Remember what role that person who led you the most into the loving arms of the Lord played in your salvation. Now when you remember that, imagine where you would be had that person not been there. This is the only motivation we should ever need to open our hearts, mouths and lives up to another person.

Actively seek opportunities to share the message of what Christ has done in your life with others. This does not mean bash them over the head with Scripture of why they are wrong in what they believe. This means look and be ready for any opportunity you might have to answer their questions or share with them the hope and love you now have in Christ Jesus. Often, though, this may require the use of Scripture as credibility for your points and possibly for confronting sin.

There is nothing greater on this earth or in this existence than to help someone come into the loving arms of the Father through the grace of Jesus Christ! This is the only act or deed we can participate in on earth that will help usher someone into the eternal kingdom of Christ. Anything else we do for someone is temporal, fleeting. But leading someone to the open hands of Christ and His cross will continue on forever.

Lastly, don't feel apprehensive or unsure about yourself when confronted with the idea of sharing the gospel. Take heart in the fact that you are sharing a personal experience, which can never be debated! You should also take the biggest confidence and peace in knowing that the Lord Jesus is with you always! His Spirit is in the midst of your words and in the heart of your message.

So go and tell the world!

Prayer:

Most giving and gracious Father God we thank You for the redemption and salvation we have through the loving and scarred hands of our Savior Jesus Christ! Father God help us to never take for granted the deliverance we have in You! And let us never forget the freedom we now have to love and share Your love with those who are lost and hurting! Fill us, Father God, with the loving Spirit that You showered onto each of us through the cross of Calvary. Give us the strength and assurance that You are with us as we seek the message of Hope that You have given us in the mercy of Your holy gift of being crucified with Christ. May we never lose sight of the fact that our life is not our own any longer, but is found in You and Your forgiving kindness. Grant us the desire and burning passion to see others come to You and Your salvation as You showed us in the Garden of Gethsemane. May we be Your shining Light through the beacon of sharing the gospel. In the mighty and glorious name of Christ and for His glory always, Amen!

Chapter Thirteen
I AM with you always: Discipleship

> *"So then you are no longer strangers and aliens, but you are fellow citizens with the saints, and are of God's household, having been built on the foundation of the apostles and prophets, Christ Jesus Himself being the corner stone, in whom the whole building, being fitted together, is growing into a holy temple in the Lord, in whom you also are being built together into a dwelling of God in the Spirit."*
> —The Apostle Paul

> *"But the goal of our instruction is love from a pure heart and a good conscience and a sincere faith."*
> —The Apostle Paul

We have now come to the end of our journey together, upon this particular occasion, and yet have reached the very beginning of your journey with the Guide: Jesus Christ. Up until now we have looked into the ways that we can pursue the presence of God, apply the grace of God to our daily life and even learn how to live a life of love.

And it is within this last part, part four, that we finally climb to the peak of the Christian life; we reach our highest goal of the life in the Spirit. All of the spiritual disciplines, fruits of the Spirit and guidelines outlined within this book aim towards accomplishing the same uniform purpose: our every single breath and movement as believers and servants of the Lord of lords are designed to mold us into becoming the reflected image of Jesus Christ.

He intends to shine up this mirror known as us so that when He looks into the crystal surface He sees His face staring back. But what does that process entail? What is the ultimate expectation of Christ once we have firmly established that we love God with all of our being and love others as ourselves in every aspect of our daily lives? Let us take one more look at the character and nature behind Jesus. The face of Christ is one that definitely inspires disciples, strengthens disciples and leads disciples but especially, *makes* disciples, hence why this final chapter immediately *follows* evangelism. Leading an individual to Christ is not the end of their spiritual growth, their journey…or yours.

The true purpose of becoming a disciple of Christ is indeed to perfectly reflect the crystal clear image of Christ and to not only become more like Him, but to become more like Jesus than ourselves. Yet this purpose is not an end in and of itself but a new beginning. Christ intends to make us a new creation so that we might begin life anew for Christ, for ourselves and for others! You see, a mirror perfectly reflects the actions of a person's movements. A reflection does not move on its own but follows, in perfect harmony, with the movements of the person facing the mirror. We are all to be a mirror unto the movements of Jesus Christ. We are to be His reflected movements in all that we do.

I know that this seems as either impossible or crazy, but as we have discovered throughout this expedition: nothing is impossible when it comes to living your life in Christ. This life in Christ will always be crazy to us as long as we're on this side of heaven! And it is that craziness that makes the Christian life so amazingly beautiful and fulfilling. We are truly born again, born anew into an altogether miraculous life when we become children of the most High God through our Savior, as C.S. Lewis states:

And now we begin to see what it is that the New Testament is always talking about. It talks about Christians 'being born again'; it talks about them 'putting on Christ'; about Christ 'being formed in us'; about our coming to 'have the mind of Christ.'

[...] They mean that a real Person, Christ, here and now, in that very room where you are saying your prayers, is doing things to you. It is not a question of a good man who died two thousand years ago. It is a living Man, still as much a man as you, and still as much God as He was when He created the world, really coming and interfering with your very self; killing the old natural self in you and replacing it with the kind of self He has.

At first, only for moments. Then for longer periods. Finally, if all goes well, turning you permanently into a different sort of thing; into a new little Christ, a being which, in its own small way, has the same kind of life as God; which shares in His power, joy, knowledge and eternity. [44]

Discipleship has only one, crazy goal: to make you so much like Christ that you are indeed a portrait of the life, love and *work* of God. This goal encompasses many, many aspects of a lifetime of transformation, but still purposes one thing: to make us, no matter the pain, time or cost, into the very likeness of the Living Lord and to *aid* in *the transformation of others!*

Hallelujah!

The Blessed Opportunities of Discipleship

Discipleship is our opportunity to help build up and edify other children of God so that they might follow the Lord Jesus more intimately and seek Him more passionately and eagerly. This process involves three specific opportunities we must seize to adequately help make authentic disciples of Christ: *encourage a child of God, hold accountable a follower of Christ* and *edify our brother and sister in the Lord* as they become their own reflection of Jesus: a disciple-maker!

Opportunity One: Encouraging a Child of God

The word "discipleship" really entails a mode of learning and change that happens to a person through the guidance and teachings of another individual. Yet Christian discipleship is unique in that the "learnee and changee" is not really following the guidance and teachings of their mentor or discipler, but Christ through them. Immediately, you might begin to see why the very essence of Christian discipleship is a bit more complex and complicated than we probably realized or ever even contemplated.

It is a fine line all Christians walk when they are aiding in the discipleship of another. This fine line is comprised of exercising authority as a representative of the Lord while not overstepping the bounds into presumptuous self-righteousness, teaching lessons and Scriptural truths without lecturing and scolding. Lastly, the fine line involves lovingly confronting someone while abstaining from rebuking and berating them. Tricky, huh?

In fact, this might even seem like it's more of a burden than a blessing. It actually is a burden, to a degree. The Word of God commands each of us to build each other up in Christ and invest our gifts and talents into each other so that the entire body of Christ (the church) might glorify the Lord and lead others into the loving hands of the King. But what a blessed privilege and opportunity that is! There is no greater blessing than to assist in the transformation of a fallen, wayward soul into the pristine, exalted image of Christ.

Encouraging a child of God is the first step in the process of discipleship quite simply because this may be the hardest one of them all in practice, not theory. In theory it's simple and easily performed. You inspire them to grow in the Lord and lift them up when they fall or grow weak and weary. But the actual practice of that theory is a delicate process of honest support, investment of time with emotional attachment and tender comfort.

Can you begin to see the true wonder that encouraging a child of God entails; so much to accomplish within a minefield of possible mistakes and misunderstandings. Yet, this marvelous action perfectly demonstrates the awe and splendor that Christ is to each of us. This reflection of Jesus' divine encouragement despite being in such a volatile environment can't help but aid the transformation of a soul into the image of Christ.

So let's look at the ways that we can encourage a fellow child of God.

First, you can support a child of God in their pursuit of the Lord Jesus.

Support their growth by inviting them to become involved in groups, events or material that can present them with the spiritual disciplines discussed, you can bring them into the presence of other brothers and sisters in Christ who can help disciple them as well and, of course, by doing all of this you will bring them into the presence of the Holy Spirit who is *the* Discipler.

The most important thing to comprehend when attempting to make disciples of Christ is to realize that you can not and will not effectively disciple them alone. You can't, and any attempt to do so is an exercise in futility. You need help and with good reason: we are all the body of Christ and thus have been designed with our own individual gifts to build each other up in a special and unique way. You have a specific role to play in the discipleship of another child of God but so do others; so take advantage of the wonderful entity known as the church and truly support the growth of another by involving others in that support. That is what true support is: it's not an individual's hands lifting them up but the support system of a multitude of saints.

Secondly, you can comfort another child of God in their time of affliction. This is the sister-encouragement to support because this also mainly involves the full and ever-reaching power of Christ's body, the church. One of the other most important parts that the church as an entity plays in the lives of believers is the process of comforting those who mourn or are afflicted. We can not do this Christian life on our own; we were not designed to, that's a part of the beauty of fellowship. So since we know we can't do this on our own we must also acknowledge the fact that we will eventually fall and fail. We have also been given the knowledge from Scripture that we will be persecuted for our faith in Christ and face affliction. This is why the church as a body of believers must not allow ourselves to be so divided and fractured: *we need each other*!

Christ knew that the only way we could face the hardship of this life was through the power of His Holy Spirit, which speaks and moves through us in three major ways: through our hearts, through Scripture and through *believers*! 2 Corinthians 1:3-5 reveals just how vital comforting a child of God is in the process of discipleship:

"Grace to you and peace from God our Father and the Lord Jesus Christ. Blessed be the God and Father of our Lord Jesus Christ, the Father of mercies and God of all comfort, who comforts us in all our affliction *so that we will be able to comfort those who are in any affliction* with the comfort with which we ourselves are comforted by God.

"For just as the sufferings of Christ are ours in abundance, so also our comfort is abundant through Christ." (emphasis added)

The Holy Spirit comforts us to give us assurance and console us, but also so that we will comfort others in their hour of need with the same comfort we have been blessed with by God. The abundance of comfort possible in the church, by every and all believers, is a power that is not used enough today and even more incredibly, can't be conquered.

Thirdly, to encourage a fellow child of God we must invest our time and life in them. When I say this I do not mean flippantly or haphazardly, I mean an honest and sacrificial investment. When we invest in a business, house or vehicle we do not and can not do so without sacrificing our monetary stockpile. The investment from a disciple into another disciple's life is infinitely greater. We don't just invest our resources or time into them but our very life, our very essence. We give them a part of ourselves, our talents and spiritual gifts so that they may be one step closer to resembling the complete person of Jesus Christ.

This is a great sacrifice to make because it is an ongoing sacrifice. But just as all investments are risky and sacrificial, they are equally rewarding when a wise investment brings joy and gain. When you invest in another disciple they invest in you as well. They lift you up one step closer to resembling Jesus and give you all of themselves. Remember fellowship? Remember comfort from a few paragraphs prior to this one? These are all possible when children of God, the body of Christ, the very church itself invest in each other and sacrifice their lives for one another so that we might all become the reflection of the Lord Jesus Christ on this earth and for eternity!

Opportunity Two: We must hold our fellow followers of Christ accountable.

With all the intricate delicacies that making disciples entails, holding one another accountable is the most intricately delicate of them all. Why? This *blessed* opportunity, remember that it is a blessed opportunity, requires a tremendous amount of grace and righteous indignation. "What?" Yes, that's right. Accountability combines two aspects of God's character that do not co-exist easily, except within the heart of God. And it is this realization that we must not and can not overlook! Only a disciple who is intimately and deeply within the heart of God, overflowing with the tangible grace and righteous indignation of the Holy Spirit, will ever be able to hold another disciple accountable in true obedience to the will of God.

The first requirement of keeping another disciple accountable is to keep yourself accountable to the Lord Jesus. If there is a part of your heart that you have kept from the Lord or a sin stronghold you are unwilling to confront through the help of the Holy Spirit then you will be incapable of helping another disciple open all of their heart unto the Lord. You will be incapable of confronting another disciple's sin stronghold without first allowing the Holy Spirit to confront you about yours. Without this constant evaluation of self in the Spirit, the Spirit can't and won't enable you to help another believer because usually, you will be so blinded by your own sin that you can't notice the sin in your brother or sister.

The second requirement is to pray and ask the Lord for guidance. Pray about confronting them and if it is the right course to take. Now as I write this I worry that this will be used as an excuse to escape a Spirit-driven call of action to keep a brother or sister accountable. Many individuals use prayer as an escape route *out* of Christ-like action instead of as the tool and enabler that it is *for* Christ-like action. Pray for guidance in your obedient action, not the flashing neon billboard that will tell you everything, which will exclude uncertainty, as discussed earlier.

The importance of praying for the Lord to guide your words and your ways while you approach the fellow disciple can not be overstressed; again, if God is not present in the confrontation, which by all means accountability is, then the opportunity for discipleship won't be either. Also, when confronting them, do so as a friend in Christ and not as a rule-keeper or Bible-basher. If you really care about another Christian's walk in the Lord then you will be a graceful friend *and* a righteously indignant servant of God. Don't speak down to them or belittle their struggles. No, express your true concern and even sadness if so appropriate.

I have never seen a disciple of Christ become outrageously angry or offended when confronted by a concerned and loving friend about the wrong or questionable decisions of that disciple of Christ. Now there is normally pain involved, but the pain usually centers on the disciple who has gone astray because they begin to fully comprehend the ramifications of their sin and unwise decisions. Why? Because they see for the first time just what pain and distress their actions have caused an individual they care a great deal about; they experience the good guilt of God that leads to repentance and most wonderfully, renewed love and passion for Christ.

Accountability is an act that requires a great deal of selfless humility from both parties. From the confronter, because the disciple must realize that they have no room to speak about their holiness, as they are a redeemed sinner, and so must rely upon the Lord's guidance and righteous grace for guidance and strength. From the one confronted, because that disciple must acknowledge not only their faults and sin, not only acknowledge their need for change and help, but accept the advice and intervention of another redeemed sinner's disapproval and declarations.

"He whose ear listens to the life giving reproof will dwell among the wise. He who neglects discipline despises himself, but he who listens to reproof acquires understanding. The fear of the Lord is the instruction for wisdom, and before honor comes humility." Proverbs 15: 31-33

As you can see, this act must be drenched in God because without the

Holy Spirit's presence the weight of this blessed opportunity will crush the unprepared and unfilled follower of Christ. Yet when God is present in the life and the Holy Spirit is overflowing out of the heart of a concerned disciple the might of this redeeming confrontation crushes iniquity and produces powerful discipleship.

"The heart of the righteous ponders how to answer, but the mouth of the wicked pours out evil things. The Lord is far from the wicked, but He hears the prayer of the righteous." Proverbs 15: 28-29

OPPORTUNITY THREE: WE MUST EDIFY OUR BROTHERS AND SISTERS
IN CHRIST AS THEY BECOME DISCIPLERS

Where encouragement and accountability impacts disciples, edification solidifies and prepares the disciple for their own process of becoming Christ's reflection: edification builds up the disciple to be able to aid the discipleship of others. In short, edifying another brother or sister in Christ is the final step in providing them with what they need to aid in the discipleship of another brother or sister.

The genius of the church is that it is as much a living entity as are the believers who comprise it. The church is forever capable of building up disciples so that they might build up other disciples and so on and so forth. You see the final step of making a disciple is in fact already completed when we approach this final step. Huh?

Edifying a brother and sister in Christ is something you do throughout the other two opportunities of encouragement and accountability. You edify them by becoming the clear reflection of Christ, by becoming the example of how to disciple. By supporting them in their pursuit of Jesus, by surrounding them with other supportive disciples, you build them up in the truth that they can not disciple another brother or sister on their own. By comforting them in their affliction you instill in them the very power and purpose of the church: that we might all share in the abundant mercies and riches of Christ, together! By investing in their life you paint a portrait on their soul of the true nature of sacrificial discipleship, which is the model that Christ Himself gave us. You fortify their appreciation of fellowship with one another and with the Lord by revealing to them the great joy and blessing that investing their life into another disciple brings to not only themselves, but the body of Christ as a whole!

When you hold them accountable for their actions as a gracious, righteously indignant servant of God you reveal to them the truth that the Lord will not leave them in sin and thus they are commanded to not only keep themselves accountable before the Lord but to not allow their brothers and sisters to sinfully stray from the guiding footsteps of Christ either. You strengthen their resolve to live their life in the Spirit, which is the only way that they can effectively disciple another brother or sister through the grace and reproof of God.

Finally, you edify them to not sit idly by and focus only on their own growth in the Lord. You help place in them the foundation that as "little Christs," reflections of His very person on earth, we are called, commanded and compelled to help other brothers and sisters become the "little Christs," the perfect reflection of Jesus Christ that the Lord promises them they will become. You solidify within them the most Christ-like aspect of discipleship: it's not about me, it's all about Jesus. They have become, through your edification and living life in the Spirit, a rock that Jesus will use to further build up, strengthen and perfect the Temple of God: His church.

"For we are God's fellow workers, you are God's field, God's building. According to the grace of God which was given to me, like a wise master builder I laid a foundation and another is building on it. But each man must be careful how he builds on it.

For no man can lay a foundation other than the one which is laid, which is Jesus Christ…

Do you not know that you [all] are a temple of God and that the Spirit of God dwells in you? If any man destroys the temple of God, God will destroy him, for the temple of God is holy, and that is what you are." –1 Corinthians 3:10-11, 16-17 [Greek use of "you" there is plural]

Edification is about having an eternal perspective: the perspective of Christ. And within this revelation is the stunning promise of Christ when you choose Him as Lord and Savior and become His disciple: His foundation can never be destroyed; He never lets go. With Christ as our Guide and Teacher, we will become just what the Father intended us to be: holy. This glorious truth is said possibly more in the Bible than any other commandment or statement. When you turn fully and genuinely to God, He will never let you fall out of His hands but will make you like Christ:

"The Lord is the one who goes ahead of you; He will be with you. He will not fail you or forsake you. Do not fear or be dismayed." –Deuteronomy 31:8.

"Just as I have been with Moses, I will be with you; I will not fail you or forsake you." –Joshua 1:5

"My sheep hear My voice, and I know them, and they follow Me; And I give eternal life to them, and they will never perish; and no one will snatch them out of My hand.

My Father, who has given them to Me, is greater than all; and no one is able to snatch them out of the Father's hand." –John 10:27-29.

Once we answer the Voice that calls us we will forever be in the hands of Almighty God. Our life will be filled with joy, peace and an excitement that comes from having an intimate relationship with the Creator, which allows us to help others have intimate relationships with Christ, which *then* edifies them to help others have intimate relationships with Christ, etc. When we finally pursue the call of God we will find that we have been *made* whole by His presence and are *being* made perfect through the Refiner's fire. We will realize that by being made whole and finding fulfillment, we are helping to do the same to our brothers and sisters in Christ. We will discover on the day we meet Christ, that He has made us more than we ever thought we could be: His reflection, His servant and most astoundingly, His friend.

All we have to do is reflect our Lord and Savior, by following the Shepherd:

"What then shall we say to these things? If God is for us, who is against us? [...]

Who will separate us from the love of Christ? Will tribulation, or distress, or persecution, or famine, or nakedness, or peril, or sword? [...]

But in all these things we overwhelmingly conquer through Him who loved us.

For I am convinced that neither death, nor life, nor angels, nor principalities, nor things present, nor things to come, nor powers, nor height, nor depth, nor any other created thing, will be able to separate us from the love of God, which is in Christ Jesus our Lord." –Romans 8:31, 35, 37-39

Do you hear it?

Can you feel it?

The Voice is calling you to come and find the abundant and fulfilling life; the perfect life that abides only in the presence of Almighty God, only in His unfathomable love and only in intimately knowing the Lord Jesus Christ.

"Go therefore and make disciples of all the nations, baptizing them in the name of the Father and the Son and the Holy Spirit, teaching them to observe all that I commanded you; and lo, I am with you always, even to the end of the age." –Matthew 28:19-20

Application:

Follow Jesus Christ by aiding others in their pursuit of Him.

For thirteen chapters we have discussed and discovered the ways in which we can grab hold of completion by seeking the Lord. We have learned how to enter into His presence daily, apply His grace to our every moment and learn to live a life of love. So now, it is time for you to "Go!" and help others do the same. Become what Christ has commissioned you to be: a disciple-maker.

Claim the promise that Christ has for you! Become who God created you to be: a son or daughter of God! Now go out there and build up other children of God! Reflect Christ onto others so that they may reflect Christ unto the ends of the earth, even to the end of the age.

May the Lord of heaven and earth bless you and keep you and may the grace of our Lord Jesus Christ build you up and make you strong through the Holy Spirit. I will pray for you, my very loyal reader. You've made it thus far and I can't wait to see what wonderful things for the Lord and others you will do.

And I will thank God for you, my friend, for the expedition you are about to undergo and the life in Christ you lead. And one day, I look forward to seeing you in the communion of saints around His throne!

Prayer:

Most gracious and loving Father God we thank You for the gift of life that You have given us; not just the breath of life that created us but the New Life that you grant each of us if we will but turn to You. Father, please give us the strength to grasp hold of the Promise we have in Your precious Son Jesus Christ. May we always cling to Your side and do everything we can to seek You in every moment of our lives so that we might edify and build up Your children to authentically and wonderfully follow You. Bless us with Your Holy Spirit, Lord, so that we might become more like You and help others pursue You more closely and intimately. Above all, Father God, empower us to live a life that glorifies and honors You, most precious Lord, in all that we do. We ask humbly and sincerely in the wonderful and powerful name of Jesus Christ our Lord and Savior, Amen!

Appendix

"Dearest Lord Jesus..."

The prayer below helped me best put into words the desires of my heart, which were to give my life to Christ and tell Jesus that I believed in Him as Lord and Savior, wanting the Messiah to take over my life and save me.

> *"Dearest Lord Jesus, thank you for loving me Lord. Thank you for dying on the cross for my sins and transgressions. Lord, I know that I am a sinner and am unable to save myself. Lord Jesus, I believe in You. Come into my heart, Lord. I trust in You alone for salvation, Lord. Take over my life, Jesus, and save me. Thank you, most precious Jesus, for saving me!"*

On the authority of the Holy Bible, the very Word of God, if you prayed that prayer with a genuine heart and meant every word with your very soul, then as Scripture promises us the Lord Jesus came into your heart, your life and saved you! Congratulations! Scripture tells us that the angels in heaven rejoice over your salvation! As do I! Welcome to you my brother, my sister in Christ.

And now, your life, your journey truly begins anew!

Index of Bible Verses

Chapter One: Abiding in the Light of God

Matthew 7:7.
Isaiah 40:3-5.
James 4:8.
Proverbs 8:17.
Matthew 7:1.
Philippians: 4:13.
Isaiah 40:30-31.
Matthew 19:26.

Chapter Two: The Heartbeat of Christianity: Prayer

Psalm 6:9.
1 Thessalonians 5:16.
Ecclesiastes 2:11.
Exodus 34: 29-35.
2 Chronicles 32:31.
Hebrews 11:1.
2 Corinthians 5:7.
Proverbs 28:13.
1 John 3:20b.
Matthew 7:7- revisited.
Mark 11:23.
Mark 11:24.
Matthew 19:26.
Psalm 46:10a.

Chapter Three: For My Eyes Have Seen the King: Worship

John 4:23-24.
1 Corinthians 3:16.
James 4:8a.
Romans 8:26-27.
1 Corinthians 2:10.

Chapter Four: Man Does Not Live on Bread Alone: The Word of God

Psalm 119: Beth 11, 15-16.
Luke 4:1-2.
Psalm 119: 105-107, 116.
Matthew 4:4, Deuteronomy 8:3.
John 4:10-14.
John 4:15.
Ephesians 6:10-13, 16-17.
Luke 4:3.
John 4:24.
Luke 4:6-7.
Luke 4:8.
Luke 4:9-11.
Luke 4:12
2 Corinthians 1:3-5.
2 Corinthians 12:9-10.
2 Timothy 3:16-17.
Romans 12:2.
Mark: 1:15
Psalm 119:81.

Chapter Five: Clinging to the Vine: Faith

Mark 9:22-24.
Proverbs 21:2.
Romans 8:28.
Luke 22: 41-42.
Luke 23:39.
Luke 23:40-42.
Luke 23:43.
1 John 4:18-19.
Psalm 23:4.
Daniel 3 (entire chapter referenced)
John 15:5.
Philippians 4:3.
John 6:66-69.

Chapter Six: Embracing Our Weakness for His Strength: Humility Through Grace

Luke 18:9-14.
Luke 18:14.
James 4:10.
Matthew 25:23.
James 2:17.
Proverbs 16.2.
Matthew 23:25-28.
Matthew 23:10-12.
Matthew 5:3.

Chapter Seven: To Each His Own: Forgiveness

Matthew 18:23-27.
Matthew 18:28-34.
Matthew 18:35.

Ephesians 5:1-2.
Ephesians 4:25.
Luke 7:47b.
Romans 12:17-19, 21.
Matthew 18 – revisited.
Colossians 2:13-14.
Romans 2:5-6.
Matthew 7:1-5.
Romans 2:1-5.
Proverbs 22:24-25.
Proverbs 13:20.
Proverbs 27:17.

Chapter Eight: Taking Up Daily the Cross of Christ: Devotion

Luke 22:42.
John 15:10-11.
Mark 8:37.
Philippians 1:21.
Revelation 3:16.
Matthew 25:14-30
John 16:24.
Galatians 2:20.
Luke 22:42.

Chapter Nine: The Selfless Forgetting of Me: Service

1 Corinthians 4:1.
1 Peter 4:10-11.
Joshua 24:15.
John 13:8.
Luke 22:26.
Matthew 16:24-25.
John 13:12b-15.
Galatians 5:13-14.
Ephesians 4:7-13.
Romans 12:1.
John 12:25-26.

Chapter Ten: The Family of God: Fellowship

John 15:4-5, 9.
1 John 1:6-7.
Matthew 18:20.
John 17:22.
Romans 8:31, 35, 37-39.
1 John 4:16, 18.
John 17:20-26.
1 Peter 4:8.

Chapter Eleven: And the Greatest of These Is: Love

John 13:34-35, 14:15.
1 John 3:18; 4:16,19.
1 Corinthians 13:1.
1 John 4:20-21.
1 Corinthians 13 – revisited.
Proverbs 3:27.
Galatians 6:9-10.

Chapter Twelve: Go: Evangelism

Matthew 28:19-20.
Acts 8: 29-30.
Romans 1:16-17.
Acts 8:29-31, 35-37
1 Peter 3:15.
Matthew 28:19-20.
John 14:16.
John 18:38.
John 18:37.

Chapter Thirteen: I AM With You Always: Discipleship

Ephesians 2:19-22.
1 Timothy: 1:5.
2 Corinthians 1:3-5.
Proverbs 15:31-33.
Proverbs 15:28-29.
1 Corinthians 3:10-11, 16-17.
Deuteronomy 31:8.
Joshua 1:5.
John 10:27-29.
Romans 8: 31, 35, 37-39.
Matthew 28:19-20.

Bibliography

1. Manning, Brennan. *Lion and Lamb.* Grand Rapids: Chosen Books, 1986, 25, 90.
2. Ortberg, John. *The Life You've Always Wanted.* Grand Rapids: Zondervan, 1997, 106.
3. Lewis, C.S. *The Problem of Pain.* San Francisco: HarperSanFrancisco, 1996, 91.
4. Willard, Dallas. *The Divine Conspiracy.* New York: HarperCollins Publishers, 1998, 246.
5. Foster, Richard. *Pursuing Spiritual Transformation Bible Study Series: Growth–Training vs. Trying.* Reading adapted from Prayer: Finding the Heart's True Home. Grand Rapids: Zondervan, 2000, 62.
6. Spurgeon, Charles Haddon.
7. Lewis, C.S. *Letters to Malcolm, Chiefly on Prayer.* New York: Harcourt, Brace, & World, 1964, 22.
8. Ortberg, John. *The Life You've Always Wanted.* Grand Rapids: Zondervan, 1997, 96.
9. Ortberg, John. *The Life You've Always Wanted.* Grand Rapids: Zondervan, 1997, 96, 99.
10. Tozer, A.W. *Whatever Happened to Worship.* Camp Hill, Christian Publications, Inc., 1985, 13.
11. Kelly, Thomas. *A Testament of Devotion.* New York: Harper Bros., 1941, 12.
12. Tozer, A.W. *Whatever Happened to Worship.* Camp Hill, Christian Publications, Inc., 1985, 46.
13. Tozer, A.W. *Whatever Happened to Worship.* Camp Hill, Christian Publications, Inc., 1985, 122.
14. Lewis, C.S. *Mere Christianity.* San Francisco: HarperSanFrancisco, 1980, 30-31.
15. Ortberg, John. *The Life You've Always Wanted.* Grand Rapids: Zondervan, 1997, 188.
16. Ortberg, John. *The Life You've Always Wanted.* Grand Rapids: Zondervan, 1997, 183-184.
17. Lewis, C.S. *Mere Christianity.* San Francisco: HarperSanFrancisco, 1980, 45-46.
18. Ortberg, John. *Pursuing Spiritual Transformation Bible Study Series: Growth–Training vs. Trying.* Grand Rapids: Zondervan, 2000, 34.
19. O'Connor, Flannery. Quoted in Yancey, *Reaching for the Invisible God.* Grand Rapids: Zondervan, 2000, 48.
20. Yancey, Philip. *Reaching for the Invisible God.* Grand Rapids: Zondervan, 2000, 188.
21. Ross, George Everett. Quoted in Yancey, Reaching for the Invisible God. Grand Rapids: Zondervan, 2000, 52-53.

22. Yancey, Philip. *Reaching for the Invisible God.* Grand Rapids: Zondervan, 2000, 65.
23. Yancey, Philip. *Reaching for the Invisible God.* Grand Rapids: Zondervan, 2000, 65-66.
24. a Kempis, Thomas. *The Imitation of Christ.* North Brunswick, NJ: Bridge-Logos Publishers, 1999, 25.
25. Ortberg, John. *The Life You've Always Wanted.* Grand Rapids: Zondervan, 1997, 126.
26. Ortberg, John. *The Life You've Always Wanted.* Grand Rapids: Zondervan, 1997, 109, 110.
27. Manning, Brennan. *Lion and Lamb.* Grand Rapids: Chosen Books, 1986, 13.
28. Manning, Brennan. *Lion and Lamb.* Grand Rapids: Chosen Books, 1986, 17.
29. Lewis, C.S. *The Weight of Glory.* San Francisco: HarperSanFrancisco, 1980, 182.
30. Lewis, C.S. *The Weight of Glory.* San Francisco: HarperSanFrancisco, 1980, 177-178.
31. Lewis, C.S. *The Weight of Glory.* San Francisco: HarperSanFrancisco, 1980, 181-182.
32. Lewis, C.S. *The Problem of Pain.* San Francisco: HarperSanFrancisco, 1996, 44.
33. Lewis, C.S. *The Problem of Pain.* San Francisco: HarperSanFrancisco, 1996, 90-91.
34. Lewis, C.S. *The Problem of Pain.* San Francisco: HarperSanFrancisco, 1996, 89.
35. Open Doors USA. June 2005. *Open Doors.* 14 June 2005 <http://www.opendoorsusa.org/Display.>
36. Ortberg, John. *The Life You've Always Wanted.* Grand Rapids: Zondervan, 1997, 115.
37. Foster, Richard. *Celebration of Discipline.* San Francisco: Harper & Row, 1978, 113-114.
38. Chambers, Oswald. *My Utmost for His Highest.* Grand Rapids: Discovery House Publishing, 1992, December 12.
39. Manning, Brennan. *Reflections for Ragamuffins.* San Francisco: HarperSanFrancisco, 1998, 183.
40. Lewis, C.S. *Mere Christianity.* San Francisco: HarperSanFrancisco, 1980, 119-120.
41. Chambers, Oswald. *My Utmost for His Highest.* Grand Rapids: Discovery House Publishing, 1992, June 16.
42. Chambers, Oswald. *My Utmost for His Highest.* Grand Rapids: Discovery House Publishing, 1992, April 30.
43. Chambers, Oswald. *My Utmost for His Highest.* Grand Rapids: Discovery House Publishing, 1992, October 18.
44. Lewis, C.S. *Mere Christianity.* San Francisco: HarperSanFrancisco, 1980, 191-192.

Permissions

Scripture quotations taken from the New American Standard Bible®, Copyright © 1960, 1962, 1963, 1968, 1971, 1972, 1973, 1975, 1977, 1995 by The Lockman Foundation Used by permission. (www.Lockman.org)

Brother Andrew and Open Doors USA quotations used by permission. (www.opendoorsusa.org)

All quotes taken from *Life You've Always Wanted* - Expanded Edition by John Ortberg; Copyright © 1997, 2002 by John Ortberg. Used by permission of The Zondervan Corporation.

All quotes taken from *Reaching for the Invisible God* by Philip D. Yancey; Copyright © 2000 by The Zondervan Corporation. Used by permission of The Zondervan Corporation.

All quotes/material taken from *My Utmost for His Highest* by Oswald Chambers, edited by James Reimann, copyright © 1992 by Oswald Chambers Publications Assn., Ltd. Original edition copyright © 1935 by Dodd Mead & Co., renewed 1963 by the Oswald Chambers Publications Assn., Ltd. Used by permission of Discovery House Publishers, Box 3566, Grand Rapids MI 49501. All rights reserved.

All quotes from *Lion and Lamb* by Brennan Manning; Copyright 1986 by Chosen Books. Grand Rapids, MI 49501. Used by permission of Chosen Books "fair use" policies. (www.chosenbooks.com)

All quotes taken from *Reflections for Ragamuffins* by Brennan Manning; Copyright © 1998 by Brennan Manning. Used by permission of HarperCollins Publishers.

Reprinted from *Whatever Happened to Worship* by A.W. Tozer, copyright © 1985 by Christian Publications, Inc. Used by permission of Christian Publications, Inc., 800.233.4443, www.christianpublications.com.

Mere Christianity by C.S. Lewis copyright © C.S. Lewis Pte. Ltd. 1942, 1943, 1944, 1952.

The Problem of Pain by C.S. Lewis copyright © C.S. Lewis Pte. Ltd. 1940.

The Weight of Glory by C.S. Lewis copyright © C.S. Lewis Pte. Ltd. 1949.